DEVIL IN THE DEATH ZONE

DOM PICKETT

Devil In The Death Zone by Dom Pickett

Some names have been changed to protect those mentioned, and no doubt their recollection years later may differ in part from mine. This, however, is a book of my memory of the events that unfolded, and I have done my best to turn these memories into a truthful story.

Map illustration Abi Pickett

ISBN: 978-1-0684192-0-1

There are lots of people who have assisted me along the way but by far this book has to be a tribute to my wife Abi who has supported me throughout, both on and off the mountain. Not least, letting me go to Everest just five weeks after the birth of our first child.

Thank you for the support and freedom to pursue my dreams.

CONTENTS

EVEREST NORTH ROUTE

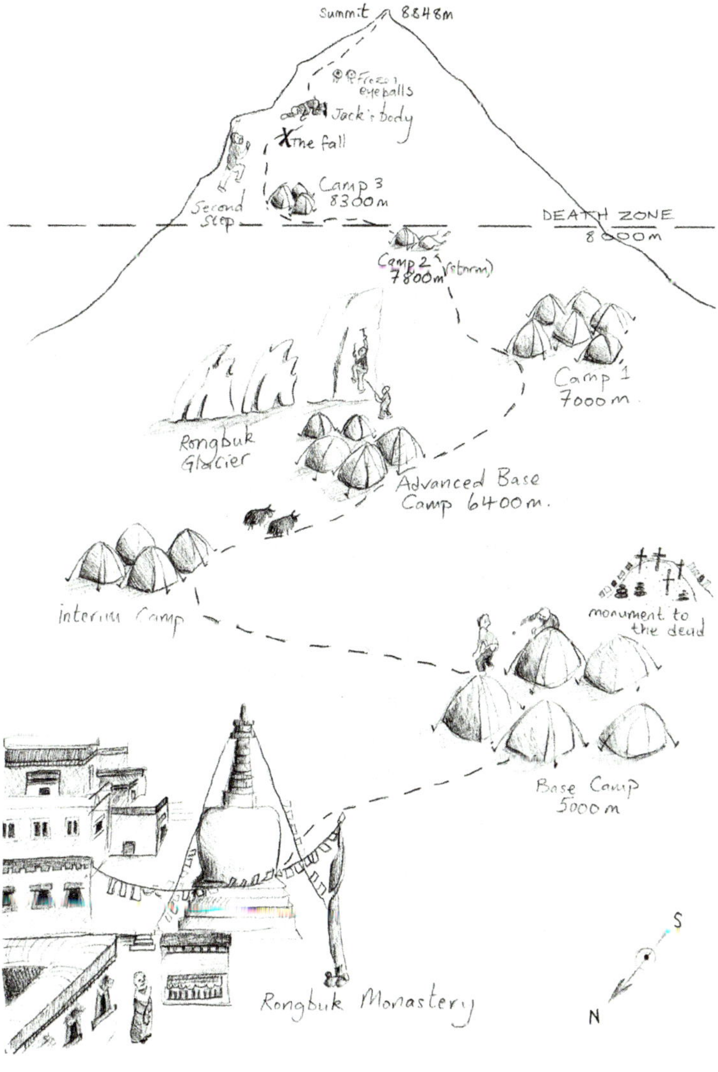

CHAPTER 1

Summit Night

I know I'm pushing too hard. I won't last another hour if I keep this pace up.

But I can't slow down. Fear and a desperate need to put this nightmare behind me drive me forward like a man possessed. Each pause to catch my breath only serves to remind me of the precariousness of my situation, a reminder made all the more agonising by the simple fact that I chose to be here.

Gazing upwards into the darkness, my flickering head torch barely illuminates the 300 ft near vertical ice gulley ahead. Systematically, I drive my ice axe and crampon points into the icy snow, inching my way up. As I pull myself over the rim, the jagged rock tears through my one-piece down jacket, sending a searing pain coursing through my torso. Ignoring the pain, I swing my right arm, planting my axe into the hard ice so as to secure myself. But something feels off this time; there's an obstruction preventing the sharp point from penetrating fully.

I'm exhausted and gasping for breath. My oxygen mask is malfunctioning, and it feels like it's smothering me. Desperate to breathe, I tear off the mask and inhale whatever I can from the thin air, trying to quell the fire in my lungs. The moisture around my mouth instantly freezes, and I feel the bite of the minus 30-degree temperature against my exposed face. I struggle to control my breathing, and as I do, I sense something beside me. Turning my faint headtorch to the left, I freeze. To my horror, the dim light slowly reveals a half-buried man in the snow. As I scan the partially submerged body, I find myself staring into the frozen eyes of a dead climber. I steady myself by tightening my grip on my ice axe, only to realise that its front point is lodged directly in his frozen stomach, hidden beneath the snow. After a few seconds, I gather myself and carefully wiggle the axe from side to side, freeing its cold steel point from the body.

I start moving upwards, eager to forget the horror I just witnessed. Then, about 50 metres ahead, I see a faint glimmer of red light. I approach, trying to determine what or who it could be. Suddenly, a shrill, strange scream echoes around the mountain, a sound that will haunt me forever.

Now high up in the Death Zone, I stare into the dark 3,000 ft abyss below me and mutter to myself through frozen lips, not for the first time on this Everest expedition, "Why am I here?"

CHAPTER 2

The Joker

After 3 years in the planning, I was finally going to start my Everest Expedition and before long, I was landing in Nepal with my massive amount of climbing kit in tow.

I had been to Kathmandu many times before. After joining the police in 2003, I quickly discovered that my day job lacked the adventure I craved. Over the years, while working in the police force, I took all my annual leave to lead groups on expeditions around the world. Nepal, the epicentre for serious climbers aiming for challenging peaks, drew me in repeatedly. Whenever I could negotiate some time off work, usually twice a year, I would lead a group of novice adventurers to various peaks in Nepal. I became well-acquainted with Nepal and its community, seeing Kathmandu as a home away from home.

But this time was different. I felt a pressure I hadn't experienced before. The familiar bars and restaurants where I used to relax, drink coffee and engage in light hearted banter now felt alien. It was as if I were a first-time tourist, eyes wide as I took in the city. I was far out of my comfort zone, facing a climb higher than I had ever attempted. Doubt crept in; I wasn't sure if I was up to the task. With all the build-up back home, sponsors, local media, and friends, the world was watching, and I could feel it.

For someone who typically thrives under the pressure of new challenges, I found myself, for the first time in my life, feeling completely overwhelmed. This unexpected surge of anxiety severely impacted my confidence. I had become utterly convinced that I was going to die.

It was mid-March, and, in theory, I had some time to settle in and relax in the city before meeting up with the small climbing team in about one week.

On any other trip to Nepal, I would have taken this time to enjoy the vibrant city, savouring a week of relaxation. Seated on a cushion on the floor of my favourite Buddha bar in Thamel, Kathmandu's bustling traveller hub, I was enveloped by the scents of incense and the chaotic symphony of honking traffic. Yet, this time, an intense and unfamiliar sensation washed over me. It felt as though I were observing my life from a distance, disconnected from my own experiences. As I ordered my favourite Paneer cheese curry with plates of freshly buttered naan to soak up the rich sauce, I couldn't shake off the thoughts of the daunting challenge ahead and the precarious situation I found myself in. A seed of doubt took root in my mind, growing despite my efforts to remain focused.

As I peered out of the window, I watched the endless rickshaw near-misses on the street outside. Somehow, injury or death was always avoided at the last second, only for the dance to begin again, relentlessly tempting fate.

As I watched a Nepalese mother cradling her infant, weaving

through the chaos of midday rickshaw traffic, a profound sense of loss and despair washed over me. Their love was visible as they navigated the perilous gauntlet. If she made one wrong move, they would perish together, a thought that churned my stomach with its stark reality. With her dark red sari, vibrant against the dusty street, she transported me back to just a few days ago, when I gazed at my own young family before leaving them behind.

Just 48 hours ago, in the dim light of a rainy March evening in England, I found myself staring through a window, transfixed by the sight of my wife cradling our newborn child. That was my final glimpse of them as the coach pulled away from Birmingham station, heading towards Heathrow. My wife waved back, though I could sense her deep, unspoken fear: would I ever return?

My mind had been on bigger things, and as the coach pulled away, my thoughts were fixated on the conquest of Everest, as they had been for the last three years. Seeing the red sari mother and her child outside the bar window overwhelmed me, and the sprouting seed of doubt was taking root. "What the hell was I doing leaving my wife and five-week-old son for what now felt like a death mission? I might as well have bought a one-way ticket."

With just under a week left in Kathmandu before meeting the team, I found myself speculating about my future companions. I conjured up images and stories in my mind, imagining what they might look like and pondering their mountain experience.

In terms of climbing experience, I considered myself quite accomplished. I had tackled numerous altitude climbs on various mountains around the world and had plenty of technical rock climbing under my belt. I had spent countless hours honing my skills on the 300 ft limestone slabs beneath the iconic suspension bridge in Bristol. Yet, despite my extensive background, there was a significant gap in my experience: I had never climbed above 7,000 metres. In the world of mountaineering, anything over 8,000 metres is considered a real challenge. The altitude alone at these heights is the biggest killer. With Mount Everest standing close to 9,000 metres (8,848 m), my true altitude experience was lacking considerably.

My solitary week in Kathmandu dragged on, each day blending into the next. Despite my best efforts to stay positive, my mind kept circling back to my glaring lack of experience at extreme altitudes. The fear of being exposed as the weak link in a team of seasoned climbers gnawed at me. With each passing day, as the team's meeting drew nearer, my confidence eroded further.

In an effort to counteract this negativity and stop myself from brooding in the Buddha bar all day, I decided to get out and see the city.

Kathmandu is a lively and bustling hub, teeming with energy. The city's vibrant traveller scene, with its abundance of bars and restaurants, offers an enticing blend of cultures and stories. It's a place where climbers and trekkers converge, sharing tales and preparing for the challenges ahead. As the gateway to the Himalayas, Kathmandu is saturated with climbing shops, each brimming with the essential gear and clothing needed for any altitude expeditions. A lot of the outdoor clothing is made to a varying degree of quality, and so the shelves of the shops are stacked high with often poorly made items with bad attempts such as "NORTH FARCE" printed on flimsy jackets proclaiming to keep you warm high in the mountains. But there are hidden gems. If you find the right shop that sells quality items, such as Shona's in the Thamel area, you can get a lot of gear at a fraction of the cost you would pay at home.

After completing the final preparations and gathering the last bits of equipment, I sought distraction by exploring some of Kathmandu's tourist sights. One of the most notable is the Monkey Temple, a stunning Buddhist sanctuary perched on a hill in the heart of the city, teeming with playful monkeys. On my first visit, a clever monkey outsmarted me by stealing my bottle of Coke. Determined to outwit it, I returned the next day with a cunning plan: tie a string to the bottle and hold onto it. Confident, I ascended the steps, only to be outmanoeuvred by another monkey who snatched the bottle and string together.

This playful diversion provided a temporary escape, but it couldn't mask my underlying apprehension about meeting the group and the looming climb. My logical side tried to maintain calm, believing that overthinking could be detrimental. Yet, in this empty week, despite my efforts to suppress it, I couldn't ignore the doubts creeping in. Scenarios of potential accidents on the mountain played out in my mind, adding to my mounting anxiety.

Each night, as I lay in my humid, damp, budget hostel, nightmares gripped me, waking me in a state of sweat and engulfing fear. With no one to share my dark thoughts with except a small band of mosquitoes, this first week marked the beginning of my descent into terror regarding my capabilities to climb Everest. An overwhelming fear of death consumed me. I kept picturing anonymous and indifferent bureaucrats making logistical arrangements to contact my wife as I lay lifeless on the side of a mountain. As the week progressed, alone, I allowed this irrational fear to spiral out of control. By the end of the week, when I was due to meet the team, I was almost ready to call it quits.

Meeting the team for the first time was a strange experience. Essentially, it's a group of strangers coming together to spend three months on the windswept plateau of Tibet to tackle the highest mountain on Earth. This was the team that would be putting their lives in each other's hands, ultimately there to save each other without question if the need arose. So, saying there was a bit of pressure on the first meeting is an understatement. I needed them to believe in me, not just for their benefit but to boost my own drained self-confidence as well.

In my head, it surely was only a matter of time before the other climbers realised I was an imposter, the Joker of the pack.

The day of the team meeting had finally arrived. After my simple breakfast of chapati and a boiled egg, I spent the morning in my room, ridding it of the last of the blood-filled mosquitoes that had been my unwelcome companions for the past week. Eventually, realising I could put it off no longer, I left my hotel.

Venturing deeper into the labyrinth of narrow streets, the tourist shops gradually disappeared, revealing the authentic face of Kathmandu. Small window shops bustled with metalwork, and the aroma of simple street food filled the air. After half an hour of walking in circles and dodging chaotic rickshaws, my weary eyes finally spotted the Panjib Guest House. This faded pink, four-storey building seemed to be held together by the web of precarious electric cables that fed into it from all directions.

I slowly ascended the four flights of stairs, passing a family with children eating their chapati and chickpea curry lunch on the ground floor landing. The stairs were filthy, with cream-coloured paint peeling off in large chunks, leaving water-stained patches that spoke of neglect and an impending sense of decay.

This was the first hint of what lay ahead. I had signed up for a budget Everest expedition, and the conditions of our initial meeting place confirmed my fears. The dilapidated state of the building was a stark reminder that cutting corners came with a price. The atmosphere did nothing to quell my anxiety; instead, it heightened my apprehension about the journey that awaited me.

On the fourth floor, I knocked on a large blue wooden door, half-expecting a Nepalese family to answer and stare at me. Instead, a tall, well-built man with blonde hair opened the door, greeting me with a friendly smile and a relaxed Dutch accent. He introduced himself as Bas, the leader of the expedition. His big, wide blue eyes put me instantly at ease. I often wonder how I appeared to him during this initial meeting. I had grown a beard over the past year to help with the Himalayan winter cold, and after a sleep-deprived week, I must have looked quite dishevelled, perhaps not as welcoming as Bas.

As he ushered me in, I realised I was the first to arrive. The room was filled with endless coils of rope and climbing gear scattered across the floor and boxes stacked high against the walls, brimming with food supplies. Bas had a knack for making people feel comfortable, and soon, I found myself recounting the interesting week I had just experienced. However, I was careful not to fully disclose my mental state.

Then, one by one, the rest of the team trickled in, all entering the room slightly wired and on edge, as I had done, not being quite sure if it was the right door that they had just knocked on.

As a tight-knit group of eight climbers, our small team quickly bonded, exchanging introductions amid smiles that concealed underlying assessments of each other's capabilities. Unspoken but palpable, the sobering reality of Everest's dangers loomed over us, reminding us that not all would return from this perilous journey. In this room, amidst these fellow adventurers, lay our best hope for survival.

It was a good mix from around the world, with Bas from Holland, Maverick, Max and Seb from the United States, Marcus from Ireland, Stephan from Germany, and Alex and I from England.

In our group, each of us boasted a diverse background in mountaineering. Marcus is poised to potentially make history as the youngest Irishman to conquer Everest at the age of 25. He seemed like a quiet character but with a strong build and a dry sense of humour. I instantly warmed to him.

Alex was a bit older, in his late 30s, with balding hair and a slim build.

From his hometown in Cornwall, nestled in the South West of England, Alex harboured a fervent ambition: to etch his name as the first Cornishman to conquer Everest's summit. Initially, I dismissed his aspiration as a joke, yet his unwavering determination swiftly dispelled any doubts. With his Cornish black cross pirate flag stowed among his gear, Alex was poised to stake his claim on the world stage. As I bantered about being the first Bristolian atop

Everest, I soon realised my mistake. Alex's pride in his Cornish heritage ran deep, and I swiftly tempered my jests to avoid causing offence. This exchange afforded me a glimpse into Alex's character; beneath his affable exterior lay a steely resolve and motivation on the climb ahead, not messing around.

All in all, though the team was a pretty relaxed bunch, and we had our mutual frugality in common in terms of opting for the more 'affordable' Everest expedition.

Seb, our expedition's senior member at his late 50s, brought a stroke of fortune to our team as a seasoned doctor. His presence was particularly advantageous, considering the usual exorbitant costs associated with having medical expertise on such ventures. Seb was mild mannered and easy to talk to. That made him approachable, fostering easy communication within the group. He had trained and specialised in kidney disease medicine but had a wealth of general medical knowledge behind him. Remarkably, it marked his second attempt after an earlier setback. During our preparatory training sessions, Seb candidly shared his experience of reaching 7,500m on Everest previously, only to no longer hold his nerve, explaining how losing your nerve on Everest can be a fatal mindset.

This time, he told me, he was prepared to risk it.

Seb was good to chat with and very candid about his previous experience.

Stephan, the lone German on our team, was a very nice guy who seemed relaxed and open to be around. Despite this, he consistently seized every opportunity to recount his harrowing Everest expedition from the previous year. During our morning coffee sessions, Stephan vividly described his final summit bid with his climbing partner, Paul. He recounted how Paul, after departing from Camp 3 into the Death Zone, encountered unforeseen challenges. Stephan detailed the moment when Paul, shortly after descending from the summit, tragically lost his vision, a chilling manifestation of severe altitude sickness. As Stephan explained, this loss of vision amidst the unforgiving terrain is not uncommon and indicates a grave condition. The increased pressure from excess fluid on the brain leads to an ever-increasing breakdown in your body, ranging from impaired sight to coordination, and eventually coma and death. Paul's demise that fateful morning, high in the Death Zone, left Stephan stranded at Camp 3 with frostbitten hands, grieving the loss of his friend, knowing that Paul would never return.

I was beginning to think I was crazy just for being here; I couldn't even begin to explain why Stephan was here to re-embark on that terrible dance and risk it all again.

Stephan's narrative, though compelling, echoes a common tale among climbers drawn back to Everest's unforgiving slopes despite repeated setbacks. His experience mirrors that of many who, initially shattered by failure, find themselves inexorably drawn back to the mountain's challenge. The allure of Everest, it seems, is not easily shaken off; even as they yearn to put the past behind them, climbers like Stephan find their thoughts returning again and again to the towering peak, reigniting a powerful obsession. I've encountered individuals who have lost a decade of their lives and mortgaged their houses on this elusive quest, driven by the fleeting dream of standing on the highest point on Earth.

I've even had people say the same about me when I was close to departure. At the time, I couldn't see the sacrifices I was making to achieve my goal. But without this drive of complete determination and obsessiveness, the dream of climbing Everest remains just that, a dream.

Stephan spoke fondly about his late friend Paul and, unable to bring him down, hoped to return to the body and retrieve some personal effects for Paul's family. It's a well-documented fact that many bodies remain high up on Everest. Anything above 8,600m, well into the Death Zone, makes it almost impossible to remove a body. The logistical challenge of organising an expedition solely for body recovery, coupled with the obvious dangers and a price tag running into the hundreds of thousands, inevitably means the place where they drew their last, hard-fought breath is where they will lie forever.

Due to the limited routes on Everest and the freezing temperatures that prevent decomposition, climbers inevitably encounter the frozen bodies of those who perished decades ago.

This haunting image had already taken root in my fragile mind, imagining the necessity of stepping over the dead to continue the ascent. This unsettling vision would soon prove a very true prediction of things to come.

Stephan went on to explain that his deceased friend Paul was a serving policeman from the UK. The fact that I was also a police officer from the UK was a minor coincidence, but one that wreaked havoc on my growing paranoia. Later that night, when alone again with my mosquitoes in my hovel of a hotel, I was taking everything as a bad sign of things to come.

Maverick was very much your all-American type, with a strong build and even stronger accent; he enjoyed recounting the ill-fated expedition on Everest's north side the previous year with Stephan and Paul. Although Maverick had not actually been there, he couldn't stop talking about death. Brash and assertive, he was quick to claim that unless you'd climbed over 8,000 metres, you had achieved nothing of physical significance. He insisted that the true test lay in high-altitude climbing and often emphasised that those untested in the Death Zone were likely to perish.

Such was the mood during this preparation period in Kathmandu that I found myself waking up every night with a start, haunted by a recurring nightmare of slipping off the mountain and screaming as I fell into the cold abyss below.

The physical weight I had intentionally put on for Everest, an extra 3 stone, knowing I would need it for the coming months in the remote Tibetan Himalayas, was starting to drop off me within just two weeks in Kathmandu. My fear was so intense that I couldn't eat, a state I had never experienced before. I kept reminding myself that this was not like me.

I needed to get out of here. In my head, I had worked out my survival exit plan. I needed a way of getting off this death train I was on and was convinced it was heading towards only one certain hellish outcome.

CHAPTER 3

Obsession

The pressure to succeed on Everest was immense. With the local media back home, professional sponsors like Vango, and the financial support from the police, friends in the climbing community, and family all invested in this obsession, I needed to come up with something; I couldn't just quit.

Instead, I devised a plan to go over to Tibet with the team for the climb. Given that we were in the remote wilderness of Tibet, it was impossible to arrange a return trip without prearranged transport, which cost thousands. Then, an idea struck me: there would be a transport opportunity midway through the expedition when we received a supply drop. My plan was to climb only as far as the North Col on Everest, at 7,000 metres. Although this section was challenging, with a 500-metre ice wall, it was relatively safer at that altitude. Upon reaching this point, I could inform the group that I intended to return home with the now-empty supply vehicle. This way, I would have some stories and a minor achievement to go back home with.

Deep down, I knew the truth behind the facade I was crafting. Over the years, I've realised that no one really cares about the specifics of your journey up the mountain. The only question they ever ask is, "Did you make it to the top?" Anything less than that, even if you're just 50 metres shy of the summit, doesn't count in their eyes. All the stories and justifications you create don't matter; they're not really listening.

It took a strongly worded email from my wife, Abi, back in the UK to start setting me straight and getting my mind partially back on track. She reminded me of my past triumphs, like Special Forces physical selection and swimming the English Channel. I had doubted myself then but still pushed through, she said, hoping to instil some confidence in me. Her words helped, but only enough to stave off thoughts of my demise for a few hours each night.

As we planned to climb the north side of Everest in Chinese-controlled Tibet, we had to wait for our Chinese climbing permits. During this waiting period, an opportunity arose to trek a bit, which would help us acclimatise to the altitude and get to know each other better. One morning, we decided to take a small Twin Otter aeroplane to Lukla and trek the south side of Everest in Nepal up to Base Camp. I was concerned about the extra cost, but I knew I needed to do something to change my mental state.

This well-trodden route to the south side of Everest Base camp is one I had done many times when leading groups, so I instantly felt at home.

It was our first physical endeavour as a group; we embarked on a trek that, though considered easy compared to the impending summit bid, prompted an inevitable assessment of each other's capabilities. This customary process, which happens in all spheres of life, assumed greater significance given the elevated stakes of our challenge, where we would be closely looking at one another.

Within the group, a natural division emerged. Stephan and Marcus gravitated towards the rear, maintaining a slower pace as they were generally not as fast and took longer to acclimatise to the higher attitudes. While not renowned for their swiftness, they mustered a relaxed and friendly partnership. Their voices, carried by the mountain winds, announced their approach, punctuating the serene backdrop of towering white peaks as we ascended towards base camp. Amidst the majestic Himalayan landscape, the air resonated with the jovial interplay of English, tinged with a robust Irish twang countered by a harsh German accent.

Alex and I shared a mutual affinity for speed climbing, forging a strong alliance on our initial trek. Our companionship was marked by sparse conversation but a profound understanding of our synchronised pace and stride. Throughout our training hikes, Alex emerged as a strong-fit character, his physical strength evident in every step. Our shared silence fostered a sense of contentment as we ascended together, knowing that neither of us hindered the other's progress. This unspoken harmony translated into an efficient partnership, enabling us to navigate the mountains with agility. In outdoor pursuits, such as mountaineering, speed and efficacy are paramount. Minimising exposure to harsh elements maximises recuperation time in shelter, eating food, and sleeping, ready for the challenges ahead the next day. Prioritising self-care in this manner is strategic, prolonging endurance and bolstering the likelihood of making it to the end.

Interestingly, Alex seemed to have even poorer climbing gear than I did, suggesting that his budget for Everest was tighter than mine. He consistently sported a light blue, oversized, and faded windproof top, looking like something salvaged from the lost property bin at the Royal Mail sorting office where he worked. Even now, when I recall Alex, the image that comes to mind is of him donning that faded-blue tattered coat.

The tea houses on the south side of Everest in Nepal offer a warm welcome to trekkers. Constructed mostly from hand-chiselled stone, these lodgings boast colourful guest rooms adorned with vibrant green-and red-painted wood beams and furniture. After a long trekking day, they provide a comforting refuge amidst the harsh mountain environment.

Gathered around the stove at the heart of the tea house's dining room, the familiar scent of burning yak dung permeated the air, filling my senses. Though initially unpleasant, years of trekking and climbing in the Himalayas had cultivated in me an appreciation for these moments. They signified the comforting aftermath of a hard day's trek, offering solace by the warmth of the fire.

It was here, at the end of the day, that our characters started to emerge, and the positioning within the group, consciously or unconsciously, started to take place.

Max and Maverick, both Americans, shared a history of climbing together, having conquered Cho Oyo, another 8,000m peak in Tibet. In their late 30s, they embodied the typical American mountaineer stereotype: clean-cut with a commanding presence. Their dominance was evident, often monopolising conversations with their witty banter and shared jokes. While initially entertaining and knowledgeable, they had a tendency to steer discussions to their liking. One evening, gathered around the dung fire, Max recounted a harrowing tale of Alex's near-fatal fall during their Cho Oyo expedition. It turned out that Alex and Max had met before on a previous expedition to Cho Oyo. Considered one of the easier "eight thousanders", it is still none the less a real challenge and often used to test yourself before Everest. Max talked about Alex's fall, saying he was a dead man falling seemed very callous, as if he were blaming him. His blunt delivery and apparent lack of empathy for Alex's ordeal struck a discordant note. Alex remained silent, revealing an underlying tension within the group, with Max and Maverick emerging as dominant figures.

After getting chatting with Max the following day, I asked him what he did back home in the States, where he explained that he was a motivational speaker. I mentioned I thought he might do something like that due to how he came across. I did not mean anything by this comment, but he looked at me strangely as if saying, "Who are you to make a judgement of me?"

This was the start of what I suppose was a bit of a love/hate relationship between us during the expedition.

Bas, our blue-eyed, blond-haired leader, stayed very much out of politics and chose to drink a beer whenever he could and have a relaxed conversation about the mountains.

Each of us carried a history of past triumphs, granting us the confidence to believe we could conquer this formidable peak. Despite hailing from diverse corners of the globe, we shared a singular obsession: the mountain. Our individual narratives were threaded with a series of daring adventures, each one propelling us relentlessly towards the next, culminating in our collective endeavour to confront our greatest challenge yet.

Everest was not my first obsession.

Prior to climbing Everest, there were a series of challenges that I locked my sights on and pursued relentlessly. Only now, it seems, could I clearly see that my exploits over the past ten years had formed what can only be described as a pattern of obsessive behaviour.

All crazy plans start with an idea born out of a conversation or a momentary day dream, where your mind wanders into an idyllic fantasy.

All too often, I am unaware that the seed has been planted in my head, and I'm subconsciously already laying the foundations for my next adventure without knowing it. Soon, that seed has taken root, and before long, all my energy and attention is in pursuit of my new obsession.

Many of us have these moments of dreaming where an idea is born. However, all too often, the ongoing commitment and rigours of seeing it through mean that this seed of a dream dies before it can take hold. I'm no different from anyone else on this matter; only something happens once an idea is conceived that triggers a switch, removing all obstacles and clearing a path for the idea to grow and succeed at all costs.

Once the idea of a new mission has settled and the initial excitement has died down, you then face the self-doubt of whether or not you can do it. This comes in many forms, but the strongest by far is the doubt and negativity of others towards you in achieving your goal.

Everyone has experienced this at some point where someone talks your ambition down by saying it's not worth it, it's too expensive, too dangerous or simply not possible. Beware of the doubters, as they can plant their seed within your head, destroying your original dream.

All too often, their negative doubt comes from a place of insecurity and fear, where they seek comfort in you, not realising your ambition.

For one of my first obsessive endeavours in my 20s, I decided to go big and run from Kathmandu to Everest Base camp – something that had not been attempted before. Owing to my relative inexperience, I was instantly met with the doubters stating that I was not strong enough and would fail in my attempt.

With some TV coverage surrounding the event, the pressure built with work colleagues and those outside dubious about my ability. The idea of running to Everest Base Camp had come from looking at maps and travelling in Nepal years earlier, and strangely, the doubters only strengthened my resolve. To me, the fact that so many said it was not possible, in my head it meant that if I did achieve it, then it would be a big deal. I suppose this was the beginning of me trying to make my mark. After two years of obsessive planning and training, both my friend Matt and I achieved our record of running to Everest Base Camp.

I had now proved to the doubters and myself that it could be done. It was just a case of now coming up with new ideas for adventures where all I had to do was pursue the same obsessive formula of training and single-mindedness.

Throughout my late 20s, I continued working as a mountain

guide on Kilimanjaro, gaining extra experience whilst still working in the police.

On the descent from the summit on one of my climbs, a client of mine ran into difficulty and subsequently collapsed with altitude-related issues. Being so high on the mountain, it was a real struggle to get him down. Another client, Dan, who was fairing much better, assisted me, and together, we got the injured climber down.

Further down the mountain, once all the danger had passed, Dan just dropped a comment to me, which would alter the next two years of my life. Dan had been in the Marines for the last decade and said very matter-of-factly that from what he had seen of me on the mountain; he thought I would have a good shot at Special Forces physical selection. He explained the SF reserve unit was not full-time, and so, I would not have to give up my day job in the police. And there it was, a seed had been planted. Someone who knew what they were talking about gave me an endorsement that I could do it, along with the fact that I could continue working in the police. Most importantly though, this challenge had status attached to it; an unrelenting obsession with training and pain began as I undertook SF physical selection, in an attempt to prove to the doubters and myself that it could be done.

It wasn't long before I moved on to other ideas, and instead of wanting to shoot people, in complete contrast, I decided to get into some international aid work. I had previous experience working on aid projects in Costa Rica and Nicaragua, but I knew I needed something more exciting. After getting in touch with a friend who worked in emergency response work overseas, he soon instilled a vision of working in disaster zones, and an adventurous hero's narrative was born. Before I knew it, this seed had grown, taking me through another gruelling selection course, this time in the private sector, to be a rapid disaster response worker. All of a sudden, I was away from home in the middle of an earthquake disaster zone on the Kyrgyzstan/Chinese boarder in my latest obsessed quest.

After two years and another tick in the box, I needed to get back to another physical challenge. Whilst out swimming in the sea just off north Devon, an idea popped into my head that maybe I could swim the English Channel. Not content with just being a good swimmer, I had to prove it to all with the ultimate test. I don't know where it came from, but true to form, before long, I had committed myself to my new challenge that would see me submerge myself in the freezing cold, dark waters of the English Channel. Again, having to push the doubters aside, I obsessively acclimatised myself over a year of training with constant cold showers and freezing open water swims through the winter. A year later, in a team of three, I swam to France.

Still hungry for more and not satisfied with these accomplishments, I carried on guiding mountain trips around the world; when climbing Mera peak in Nepal on a fateful moonlit night, I was mesmerised by the size of Everest standing before me. That night, the Everest seed was planted on what would be my most difficult, harrowing and ultimately my last adventure of this kind.

As our detour to the Nepal south side of Everest stretched seemingly endlessly, news finally arrived that the Chinese government had approved our climbing permits. With this welcome update, we hastened our return journey to Lukla, setting a new pace record in our eagerness to catch our flight back to Kathmandu. Finally, I felt a sense of alignment with my path and purpose. Having navigated the challenges of our hike and held my own within the group, I began to shed the self-doubt that had plagued me. Perhaps, I dared to believe, I wasn't an imposter after all. With each step, my confidence in my abilities grew stronger, a glimmer of hope amidst the daunting journey ahead.

We hastily loaded our aged Nepalese rusty green bus, its exterior adorned with crudely painted images of Hindu gods, with ample supplies and climbing gear. We packed enough provisions to sustain us for two and a half months in the remote corner of Tibet. Everything unfolded rapidly; within a mere 24 hours of returning to Kathmandu, we were ready to depart.

With each passing moment, retreat became less of an option; the investment of time and energy into realising this consuming aspiration was too substantial. The trek had a good effect on my attitude, sharpening my focus. As I sat aboard the dilapidated bus, bound northward over the looming Himalayas, I could only hope it wasn't a one-way ticket.

CHAPTER 4

Over the Himalayas

Our journey led us northward, traversing Nepal towards the Himalayan Mountain pass into China. This route, one of the few pathways across, appeared considerably improved since my last excursion with Abi a decade ago. Typically frequented by locals trading between Nepal and Lhasa, the capital of Tibet, this remote border crossing is used by a few Westerners. Hence, the arrival of eight Westerners aboard a fully loaded bus attracted the full attention of Chinese border control.

Following an arduous 12-hour wait at the border, during which the situation remained unclear, the Chinese authorities inspected each piece of our equipment. Despite possessing valid visas and permits, which appeared inconsequential to them, we found ourselves under the watchful gaze of AK47-bearing soldiers. Their professionalism was evident throughout the vigil, maintaining stoic composure despite our attempts at friendly gestures or basic Chinese greetings, which yielded no response.

Having spent a lot of time in China over the years on various trips, I learned not to interpret this behaviour as a personal affront but rather as a reflection of cultural disparities in approach.

Eventually, amidst a prolonged examination of our extensive gear, conducted without any verbal communication, they proceeded to stamp our passports, gesturing with their assault rifles as pointing sticks.

After some time, we learned the cause of the extensive search and border delay. Apparently, a group of Westerners who had entered Tibet a week prior to us had carried a Tibetan flag with them. During a routine inspection at the border, authorities discovered the flag, triggering a state of alarm and resulting in the travellers' arrest.

At first glance, the reaction may seem exaggerated for a mere flag. However, this incident is rooted in a long history dating back to the 1950s when Tibet was occupied. Since then, a persistent Free Tibet campaign has ensued, leading to the prohibition of the Tibetan national flag and any depictions of the Dalai Lama. Those found in possession of these items face severe penalties, including lengthy imprisonment.

Given the heightened political tensions surrounding Tibet and its flag, it was unsurprising that our group faced prolonged scrutiny upon being stopped. The influx of tourists carrying Tibetan flags, easily bought in Nepal, alongside numerous climbing teams converging for the Everest season, heightened the Chinese Government's apprehensions. There was a palpable fear that a climber might ascend Everest from the North in Tibet and unfurl the Tibetan flag atop the summit, a symbolic act of political defiance that would undoubtedly attract global media attention and prove a significant embarrassment for China.

Once the Chinese border guards discerned our innocence in

any such flag-related scheme, they allowed us to proceed. At that moment, my focus was solely on survival; political activism was the furthest thing from my mind. My paramount concern was ensuring a safe return rather than any aspirations of flag-waving triumph at the summit.

As we made our way through various towns in Tibet, we became a constant source of intrigue and amusement for the locals. They would gather around, captivated by our attire and climbing equipment neatly packed in our vehicles. Sometimes, they would inquire about our purpose, and we would proudly attempt to convey, through animated gestures, that we were there to climb. However, our explanation only seemed to deepen their amusement as they looked at us quizzically.

It appeared that the local Tibetans struggled to comprehend our mission. Even the renowned mountain experts, the Sherpas, seemed to have embraced the Western notion of climbing solely for the sake of it, a concept that was once foreign to them.

Over the past century, as expeditions to conquer these towering peaks commenced, Sherpas have honed their skills to perfection. Their achievements in summiting Everest now bring them acclaim and respect within their community.

However, I often found myself grappling with the notion of mountain climbing, questioning its validity. Left unchecked, the idea of ascending these perilous peaks can appear ridiculous. Indeed, in many cultures worldwide, mountaineering is still regarded as a futile pursuit. Yet, in today's world, it has become deeply ingrained in mainstream society, largely unquestioned. This was my reality, shaped by the heroic narratives of mountaineering that surrounded me during my upbringing reading of these daring adventures.

Everest, with its title as the tallest peak, always captivated me as a prize worth pursuing. In today's era of commercial climbing, where more climbers reach Everest's lofty summit, it may not be seen as the monumental achievement it once was. Despite this, it remains a significant challenge, fraught with risk and underscored by the inescapable fact that it is the highest point on Earth.

To stand on the summit of Mount Everest is still regarded by many as a big achievement, and I wanted very much to be included in this select gang. However, the motivations and reasons for climbing Everest are still very much under debate, and since the beginning, this one question has still been left unanswered: Why do I and others like me want to climb it?

Before departing for Everest, I was invited to speak at several schools in Bristol about my upcoming climb. I tailored my presentations to suit the different age groups, but it was always the younger children, around 6 and 7 years old, who surprised me the most. Being so young, they had no preconceptions as to what the norms or reasons were surrounding climbing Everest, or indeed, some had no idea what Everest was until I turned up, so it was with complete innocence and intrigue they asked the question: "Why do you want to climb it?"

I found it very hard not to answer this question without falling into some preset response you have either heard before or embellished because it sounds good.

Many phrases spring to mind and have been used over the years, such as, *"fulfilling your sense of adventure,"* or *"conquering your demons to become a stronger person,"* or *"realising a dream to be at one with the mountains in a faraway land."* Although I occasionally used these catchphrases, deep down, I knew they were far from the truth. The real reasons I was climbing Everest were much simpler, more selfish, and ultimately more human.

While sipping some boiling hot green tea in one of these small Tibetan towns, Bas just hit me with a phrase that stuck with me, encapsulating this thought. With a cool, calm Dutch accent, whilst discussing climbing big mountains, Bas just drops a comment, *"What would be even more of an achievement than just climbing Everest would be to climb Everest and not tell anyone about it."*

That night alone in my small, dirty hotel room, I was left to contemplate this thought, asking myself what the real reasons were behind me trying to summit a mountain like Everest. With so much risk and sacrifice that comes with climbing this mountain, why was I here?

The old answer that Mallory gave, *"Because it's there,"* has become an easy one that is well known and gets a laugh. However, this most simplistic of answers is probably the most accurate. It's the highest point on Earth, and as long as it remains, it will exert an irresistible pull on both readers and climbers alike. Its allure lies not just in the challenge it presents but also in the recognition and respect one earns from peers upon reaching the summit.

Lying awake in the early hours in my dark, cold room somewhere in Tibet, my mind raced. I found it hard to conclude that this climb was anything but an egotistical, status-driven pursuit.

I, too, had been captivated by the heroic tales of past explorers and the glory bestowed upon them. Perhaps that's why I was so intrigued and drawn to the uncorrupted minds of the young students, who viewed the concept of climbing Everest with fresh, objective eyes.

Having read tales of explorers like Scott of the Antarctic as a child, I was captivated by their desire to succeed and the revered place they hold in history, often overlooking the hardships and failures they faced. So consumed by the hero's narrative, I insisted my second son, Luc, take Falcon as his middle name, after Robert F Scott. The history of exploration is filled with the successes and failures of those striving to leave their mark on the world. Visiting schools, I realised I was completing the full circle of the hero's narrative that influenced me as a child. Now, I was perpetuating the false mainstream idea that these pursuits were a noble path for the greater good.

After three days of driving from the mountain border crossing and with much contemplation, we finally arrived at our Base camp on the Tibetan plateau.

The north side of Everest is accessible by 4x4 vehicles, which seems like a blessing at first since you can transport all your equipment with ease. However, this swift arrival soon becomes a curse, as it leaves your body little time to acclimatise to the altitude of 5,000 metres. By breaking the cardinal rule of not gaining altitude too quickly, you get your first real taste of altitude sickness.

In this wind-swept landscape, I found myself gasping for breath. I couldn't walk more than 10 metres without stopping, panting, and feeling an overwhelming urge to lie down. Altitude sickness manifests in various ways, but at that moment, I experienced a piercing headache that started at the back of my head and shot through my eyes like electric needles. Coupled with severe nausea and a sudden loss of balance, I was in a dire state. The best way to describe it is to imagine the worst possible hangover you have ever had and multiply it by ten.

The place we would call home for the next two and a half months was situated on a vast, open valley floor. The wind raced across this plain, sending dust and sand into our faces. Only during the brief gusts of wind could you open your stinging eyes and take in the view of the enormous, majestic, snow-capped peaks surrounding you. The entire area exuded a profound sense of isolation and remoteness. If not for the row of small tents we had just pitched, now flapping in the wind, there would be no trace of human presence.

As I look around, I notice a large mound of earth about 50 metres long, offering us some protection from the harsh Himalayan wind. I'm grateful for this small bit of luck in pitching our camp near this windbreak. However, Stephan quickly shatters any sense of good fortune by explaining that this mound is a monument to those who lost their lives on Everest. Having been here last year on his ill-fated expedition, Stephan had turned into a kind of strange, macabre German tour guide, updating me on all the notable death landmarks and whose grave is whose.

I stand before the monument, staring at the headstones of empty graves for those whose bodies still lie on the mountain, too many to count. The intense sunlight and biting wind force me to turn my gaze up the valley. Towering above me is a beast of a mountain, an intimidating giant that seems to rise endlessly. The jagged, vertical black rock and sheer ice make my first view of Everest from this side truly terrifying. Overwhelmed by its size and filled with a sense of despair, I slump onto the frozen dirt in front of the monument to the dead. As I close my eyes to fight the splitting altitude headache and waves of nausea, I'm consumed with the same single lingering thought: "Why am I here?"

CHAPTER 5

Blood Diamond

My head throbs as I flash back four years to a moonlit night high on a mountainside, where this extraordinary journey began.

In the dead of night, amidst guiding clients towards the summit of Mera Peak, a towering glacier-covered mountain nestled in the Himalayas at 6,400 metres, I turned towards the north. There, in the distance, Mount Everest loomed like a formidable giant against the night sky. Illuminated by the gentle glow of a full moon, its summit ridge reflected light, captivating my gaze as I sat, struggling to catch my breath in the rarified air.

From that moment, I was hooked. The calm ambience of the moonlit night almost rendered Everest peaceful and inviting. I often wonder how different my decisions might have been if the moon hadn't graced the sky that night or if a biting snowstorm had obscured its majestic presence, altering the course of my journey.

As the sun rose, we reached the summit of Mera Peak; a sense of accomplishment washed over us. Amidst the small celebrations, including obligatory summit photos and pats on the back, my mind had already begun to wander. A seed had been planted, taking root in my consciousness, growing steadily until it consumed my every thought, leaving little room for anything else.

A surge of exhilaration and conviction coursed through me as if all my prior exploits had converged to lead me to this pivotal juncture: the ascent of the biggest mountain of all.

Yet, this euphoria was fleeting, abruptly replaced by the harsh realisation of a glaring oversight: money. Everest, renowned for its staggering expenses, posed a daunting financial hurdle. It wasn't merely a matter of physical strength to conquer this formidable peak; rather, the insurmountable obstacle lay in the stark reality of my financial shortfall.

Idle hours at Everest Base Camp afford ample opportunity for observation. Amidst the barren expanse, you find yourself drawn, at a distance, to the intricate activities of other expedition teams. Like industrious ants, they diligently pursue their routines, each group a distinct entity marked by unique habits, clothing and equipment. Gradually, their characteristics emerge, painting a vivid picture of mountaineering life.

Most of my clothing, including jumpers, came from charity shops back home, where, for a mere £2, I could buy warm woollen garments and so make a considerable saving. However, one downside was the lack of control over colour, often resulting in various shades of pink. Despite this, I confidently donned my best second-hand pink jumper and ventured to explore neighbouring camps, keen to observe their arrangements. Over time, a stark contrast emerged between those operating on a budget and those with ample resources.

My curiosity knew no bounds, prompting me to casually drop

by their mess tents during dinner time for a cup of tea, all in the pursuit of understanding the quality of the food they were taking.

Stepping into the expansive geodesic dome tent of the Swiss expedition was a defining moment. It was here that I encountered Jack for the first time. An amiable Scottish climber affiliated with the 7 Summits Team, Jack and I quickly struck up a friendship. Interestingly, he was conducting a spying visit of sorts from his own team's setup, positioned roughly 100 metres away. Our rugged mountain attire contrasted sharply with the clean, slick appearance of the Swiss team. As we casually helped ourselves to olives and nibbles, attempting to blend in, conversations about home, family, and our shared determination to conquer the climb flowed effortlessly between us.

With our party snacks in hand, we observed the scene unfolding before us. The Swiss team's geodesic tent, towering at least five metres high and constructed from sturdy aluminium scaffolding, caught our attention. Their expedition leader, amidst the backdrop of German techno music, offered a tempting reward of $1,000 to any team member who could scale the structure from the inside, essentially climbing upside down. Jack and I exchanged incredulous glances as we witnessed this spectacle, questioning the disregard with which money was being tossed about. Soon after, a stern-looking Swiss team member approached Jack, evidently offended by our casual consumption of their snacks. With a quick excuse and a laugh, I pulled Jack away, like mischievous schoolboys escaping detention.

Every piece of high-quality equipment or better meal served on the mountain boils down to one simple factor: money.

So, what is the true cost of attempting to conquer Mount Everest? The price can be measured in countless ways, with some costs lingering as haunting memories for years to come. However, when considering purely monetary expenses, the range is substantial, spanning anywhere from the cost of a sports car to the eye-watering equivalent of half your mortgage. This vast difference depends on factors such as the chosen route and the level of support you expect to receive.

The route selected for the climb significantly impacts the overall cost. For instance, scaling Everest from the Nepalese side typically entails higher permit fees. Despite this, the allure of warmer conditions and convenient amenities, such as nearby tea houses and helicopter supply drops, often draws climbers to this southern approach.

Choosing between the north and south sides of Mount Everest presents climbers with distinct challenges and considerations. While the north side of Tibet offers a slightly more affordable option, it comes with significant logistical hurdles. The remote nature of the terrain means climbers must be entirely self-sufficient from the outset, grappling with Chinese bureaucracy to secure climbing permits and navigate border closures. Moreover, the absence of helicopter rescue services increases the risk factor significantly, heightening the stakes for climbers in the event of an accident. Consequently, the south side in Nepal emerges as the more desirable route, but with a higher price tag attached.

Once the decision is made regarding the preferred side of ascent, climbers must carefully assess the level of support they require for their expedition. Opting for a fully guided experience with a personal Sherpa, inclusive of meals, equipment, and ample oxygen supply, commands a premium price.

On the other hand, choosing a more economical approach, like I did, means embracing the challenges of the north side of Tibet. This entails assuming full responsibility for essential tasks such as cooking, water melting, and tent pitching beyond Advanced Basecamp. With a limited oxygen supply and few luxuries, climbers must prepare for a rigorous and self-reliant expedition from start to finish.

The financial demands associated with Mount Everest expeditions are immense. For those lacking the necessary funds, like myself, the journey becomes a relentless uphill battle, requiring unparalleled dedication and sacrifices, often at the expense of personal and family well-being. In many ways, the hard task of raising funds mirrors the physical challenges of scaling Everest itself.

Despite me aiming for the cheaper option on my Everest Expedition the daunting endeavour of securing additional thousands of pounds within a mere two-year timeframe is nothing short of monumental. The relentless pursuit of funds often leads to exhaustion, moments of despair, and existential questioning. Yet, amidst the doubt, I've come to understand that this journey fosters a resilience that transforms one into a more determined climber, driven by a heightened sense of self-interest and a willingness to take risks, with a clear understanding that this is your one and only shot knowing you will never be able to ever raise this kind of fund again.

On reflection, I've often contemplated the contrasting experiences of climbers who opt for the luxurious, fully-supported approach to Everest expeditions. Their emotional investment in the journey may be limited, as the comforts and conveniences provided diminish the connection to the challenge. Consequently, when confronted with the harsh realities of Everest's unforgiving terrain, the likelihood of surrendering to adversity increases significantly.

Remarkably, between 30–40% of climbers face a daunting internal struggle, succumbing to the profound challenges of loneliness, homesickness, and the looming fear of death before they even embark on their summit night ascent.

Possessing the means to own a satellite phone and reaching out to home, only to hear about the family's leisurely Sunday lunch and the warmth of a family movie by the fireplace, can evoke profound feelings of isolation while huddled in a cramped, frozen tent amidst the desolate Tibetan plateau.

During the challenging phase of questioning my purpose, I found solace in the constant reminder of the financial struggles I endured to reach this point. This thought served as a relentless motivator, compelling me to persist despite the daunting obstacles. The pain and hardship of raising such funds are etched deeply and not easily forgotten.

In the two years leading up to the expedition, I diligently pursued additional income by maximising overtime opportunities within the police force. Often tasked with the unenviable duty of arresting suspects at the shift's end I was still happy to secure extra overtime pay. I vividly recall patrolling the nightlife of Bristol, intervening in numerous pub fights, and often enduring the peril of flying glass in the small hours. Each endeavour, no matter how challenging, was driven by the singular goal of bolstering the Everest fund.

Securing a sponsorship agreement with Vango, the outdoor company, proved to be a laborious yet ultimately fruitful endeavour. Over the course of nearly six months, I diligently negotiated terms and made numerous commitments to fulfil their expectations of me as a "mountain athlete", as they put it. They however only wished to support me by giving me equipment and no hard money.

I made the most of this opportunity by placing a substantial order for mountain gear, which included a mix of tents, clothing, and camping equipment. As soon as they sent me the equipment, I swiftly transformed these items into hard cash by selling them on eBay.

However, despite these efforts, I found myself persistently grappling with the daunting gap of debt looming over my Everest climb. I was selling anything in the house that was not nailed down, £5 here and there, from old climbing gear to dusty books, each contributing a few pounds towards my goal.

Despite generating thousands from a combination of eBay sales, overtime shifts in the police force, earnings from mountain guiding, and support from small sponsors, I still found myself short of my necessary sum.

On one bone-chilling night, with temperatures plummeting to minus 30 degrees in my tent at Everest Base Camp, I huddled deep within my sleeping bag in a futile attempt to stave off the bitter cold. With only my frozen nose exposed, I couldn't help but question my decision to subject myself to such harsh conditions, yearning for the warmth and comfort of home. As I lay shivering, I berated myself for not investing in a higher-quality sleeping bag. Determined to endure the night, I fumbled through my bag in the darkness and pulled out a pair of Helly Hansen thermal leggings. I laughed to myself as I recalled how, 12 months earlier, when I was in desperation to secure funds and equipment for Everest, I had salvaged these thermal leggings from the discard pile of a famous rugby player.

In the lead-up to my departure for Everest, I seized every opportunity for paid mountain guiding work despite its modest compensation. Over the months preceding my expedition, I led numerous groups to the summit of Kilimanjaro in Tanzania, sometimes navigating large teams of up to 35 clients. While the work was demanding, the additional income, supplemented by tips, helped to bolster my Everest fund.

Ascending Kilimanjaro is not a feat to be taken lightly. Despite its classification as a trekking peak, the mountain towers nearly 6,000 metres above sea level, placing it in the realm of high altitude. With my extensive experience, having led over twenty expeditions to its summit, I've encountered the unique challenges posed by the combination of inexperienced trekkers and the thin air of altitude. This familiarity with both the mountain and the local terrain in Tanzania proved invaluable.

During one of my final trips to Kilimanjaro before embarking on my Everest expedition, I found myself guiding an extraordinary group of individuals: the last fifteen captains of the Welsh national rugby team. While they held legendary status for rugby fans in Wales, not really being into rugby, I approached the task with a sense of detachment, unfazed by their fame. My focus was solely on ensuring their successful ascent, even if it meant rousing them from their tents in the early hours of the morning to get them moving.

Among the group were Welsh icons such as the formidable Scott Quinnell and the esteemed coach Warren Gatland. Their journey up the mountain was documented in a three-part televised series titled "Captains Climb", produced by ITV.

Not only did these celeb rugby stars possess a considerable amount of money, but they also attracted a following of eager fans who sought to join them on their expedition.

In order to participate in this event, substantial financial investment was necessary, attracting a select group of affluent individuals. Following a triumphant expedition to the summit of Kilimanjaro, our return to Arusha, Tanzania, was marked by a celebratory party that spilled from the confines of the hotel onto the lively streets, where beer flowed freely, aligning with the spirited reputation often associated with rugby culture. Whilst drinking a few myself, I found myself juggling the roles of party goer and caretaker, endeavouring to maintain order. Then, whilst sipping another beer, a conversation struck about the local rare diamond called Tanzanite. It is exclusive to Tanzania and is renowned as one of the world's most prized gemstones. I had knowledge from previous visits, where I had discovered that Tanzanite diamonds could be acquired directly from the source in Tanzania at significantly lower prices.

I subtly floated the idea about the diamond to the group. To my delight, the idea piqued genuine interest among both the rugby captains and other members of our party. Recognising an opportunity to capitalise on this interest, particularly among the wealthier members of the group seeking unique gifts or trophies to commemorate their Kilimanjaro conquests or a peace offering to their wives for leaving them behind during their adventure.

I devised a plan. Armed with knowledge of the gem mines renowned for Tanzanite, located just an hour away, I foresaw the potential for substantial financial gain to bolster my Everest pot. You could buy the refined, polished version at a couple of shops in town, but I knew the margins on this would not be good enough to make it worth my while.

Among the group were two affluent CEOs and a rugby captain, all eager to acquire raw, uncut Tanzanite diamonds, enticed by the prospect of significant returns upon their return to the UK.

I gauged how serious they were and decided to give it a go.

I reached out to my trusted local contact, Dannas, familiar with his reliability in matters of security in the region. Upon explaining my intention to explore the nearby mines for the possibility of negotiating uncut diamonds, Dannas cautiously agreed, emphasising the need for vigilance as there had been incidents of buyers disappearing without a trace when deals went bad.

Within moments, Dannas appeared on his modest 125cc motorbike, his characteristic grin revealing a mixture of black, rotten, and silvered teeth. I liked Dannas, as he was always smiling and had delivered in the past, but I couldn't ignore the wariness of the locals towards him, hinting at a shadowy reputation.

Face to face, I reiterated the details to Dannas, outlining the interest from my trekking clients in procuring raw diamonds. Aware of the substantial sum involved, running into the tens of thousands, I expressed concern over the logistical challenge of arranging such a significant cash payment. Dannas, resourceful as ever, proposed an alternative route, suggesting a connection with a businessman linked to the mines who could facilitate a credit card transaction.

With the groundwork laid, I assured my eager clients to await further communication as I hopped onto Dannas's bike. Despite its limited speed, we darted forward at a brisk 20 mph, navigating the rugged terrain of dried mud and potholes that punctuated our path. Holding on tightly to Dannas, I braced myself for the bumpy journey ahead, propelled by the promise of potential riches awaiting us. I felt a metal object poking me from the rear of his jacket. I asked Dannas, "You carrying a weapon?" Dannas replied, "Always," and at that point, he pulled out his black revolver from the back of his trousers and started waving it around, shouting, "Important to have protection," with a big grin on his face, again showing off his collection of interesting teeth.

Dannas had recounted stories in the past of how he had been ambushed on his bike before and had to shoot his way out.

It felt good to know he had a weapon; I was unclear, though, whether he had any idea on how to use it.

After a long, bumpy journey, we emerged from the dense green embrace of the jungle, revealing the scars left by extensive mining. Some mines were still active, with paths leading into gaping holes 20 metres wide. Others lay abandoned as the forest began to reclaim them, with long grasses and vines obscuring the entrances. The landscape felt chaotic, as if each new hole had been dug at random.

As the day wore on, the African sun began its descent, already dipping below the jungle canopy to the west. I knew I had only about 30 minutes of daylight left; on the equator, the sun sets quickly around 6 p.m., without much warning.

Nearby, a few local men were digging. They looked exhausted, and I couldn't help but think about how tough their job was, knowing they wouldn't reap the benefits of any diamonds they found. This was a classic Blood Diamond Mine, not like the dramatised Hollywood versions with guards carrying AK-47s, but still a place of exploitation. The workers toiled under poor conditions for meagre pay, their labour enriching the mine owners while they remained trapped in poverty.

I stepped into a small, weathered hut illuminated by a harsh fluorescent light. Dannas began conversing in the local dialect, explaining our intentions to the dealer. The dealer, a stout man clad in a faded blue shirt, appeared accommodating despite the strain his bulging stomach placed on the buttons of his shirt, evidence of his years of diamond profiteering. He greeted me with a grin, leaving the office briefly and affording me a moment to contemplate my situation. As my thoughts veered towards paranoia, envisioning scenarios of being disposed of in an abandoned mine shaft, he returned carrying light-coloured fabric cloths. Seated once more, he unfurled them onto the worn wooden table before us, revealing seven stones resembling diamonds, though I remained sceptical, considering they could easily be mere quartz fragments. With a history of five years' trust in Dannas, I suppressed any doubts about being cheated. They engaged in conversation, eventually broaching the topic of price: a staggering amount was proposed. I laughed it off, hoping to convey my disbelief at the exorbitant figure while inwardly grappling with the uncertainty of my negotiation skills.

After five more minutes of negotiations, during which I tried to appear knowledgeable and serious, we finally struck a deal: My commission was set at 20 per cent. To be paid in cash.

I then called the clients, explaining the terms. They confirmed it aligned with the limited research they had managed to do in the last hour or so. Payment was processed over the phone using the credit card details of three of the trekkers. I secured the diamonds in a cloth and slipped them into my pocket. My commission, running into the thousands, was retrieved from the safe; the 20 and 50-dollar bills were counted and handed to me. I shook hands with the blood diamond boss, then quickly hopped onto the back of Dannas's bike, stuffing the small bundle of cash in one pocket and the diamonds in the other.

The sun had set completely, plunging us into darkness. The fluorescent light in the cabin made it hard for my eyes to adjust to the night outside, and it felt as if the jungle was closing in around us. Dannas was urging me to hurry.

As we roared out on the motorbike, my grip tight on the back of Dannas, a surge of self-satisfaction washed over me, with my pockets weighed down with diamonds and cash. My mind wandered to thoughts of home, but the tranquilly shattered when a figure leapt from the jungle, just twenty metres ahead. The motorcycle's headlight revealed a towering man in nothing but shorts and a t-shirt, brandishing an assault rifle aimed directly at us. The crack of gunfire echoed behind me, and Dannas swerved violently, barely avoiding a crash as he fought to regain control. A chilling realisation washed over me like a wave: we were caught in an armed ambush.

The paranoia I'd felt just moments before now became a stark reality as I faced the imminent threat of being gunned down, robbed, and discarded in one of the nearby mine shafts.

Without thinking, I reached down in front of me and attempted to extract the black revolver from the back of Dannas's trousers. It's a compact, six-round barrel pistol. As I frantically grasped and pulled at the handle of the gun lodged in the back of his trousers, the revolver's hammer snagged on the elastic band of his under pants. Dannas had partially placed the gun inside his pants, relying on the elastic to secure it in place. Unfortunately, as I wrestled the gun free, his pants came along with it, essentially granting him a "wedgy" with his own weapon. The elastic band suddenly released its grip on the gun, allowing me to aim it directly at the man wielding the assault rifle in front of me. I discharged two rounds towards him, roughly fifteen metres away. Uncertain if any bullets found their mark, I watched as he dived into the dense jungle to my left, disappearing from sight. With Dannas continuing to push forward on the bike, I swiftly pivoted towards the direction of the shots I'd heard behind me and fired two more rounds into the darkness. With my heart pounding and the handgun clutched tightly in my right hand, I held onto Dannas's shoulder with my left, fully aware that if I were to fall from this motorbike, he wouldn't stop for me. I maintained my grip on the gun, scanning the dark forest, hoping I had at least two more rounds remaining. We pressed on along the dark, uneven mud track, moving at what felt like a mere 10 mph. The feeble beam of the motorbike's headlamp cast eerie shadows, heightening the sense of dread that lurkers could be concealed within the jungle.

I found myself almost anticipating the crack of gunfire and the brutal impact of a bullet shattering my spine.

After approximately five minutes, it dawned on me that the imminent threat had dissipated, and no pursuers lingered behind. Whether this encounter was premeditated, with intentions to ambush and plunder our possessions, or merely an impromptu attempt by opportunistic individuals seeking to exploit the presence of a white guy remains a mystery to me.

The clients expressed satisfaction with their purchase despite their uncertainty about the logistics of getting the items cut and cleaned in the UK. Recognising the sensitive nature of the ambush, I made the decision to withhold the details from them. I compensated Dannas with the agreed-upon sum for his courageous efforts and encouraged him to invest in a faster bike. He jokingly requested additional compensation for the ammunition expended during the ordeal. Impressed by his calm demeanour under fire, I happily granted him some extra cash, teasingly advising him to invest in a new pair of pants. For Dannas, such encounters seemed to be just another day on the job, as he remained remarkably unfazed by the entire incident.

I, on the other hand, still needed to calm my nerves, but soon I started to feel better as I settled down to a well-earned beer, knowing that I was thousands of dollars closer to my Everest goal.

What's interesting is despite making this money, I still felt the need at the hotel that night to search through the rugby captains' discarded items of clothing and happily claimed the expensive pair of Warren Gatland's Helly Hansen thermal leggings. Now, a proud addition to my Everest kit.

Nestled within the confines of my sleeping bag at Everest Base Camp, even with layers upon layers of clothing, including my cherished celebrity thermal underwear, I find myself still shivering. It's a stark reminder not to underestimate the arduous journey that has brought me to this point. I tell myself not to overlook the countless hours of overtime and the risks I've undertaken, all culminating in this very moment.

My endeavour to gain the substantial funds required for Everest had proven to be a formidable journey, one I was determined not to abandon lightly. Enduring the biting cold within the confines of a tent on Everest, in this desolate and isolated terrain, merely represented another trial in what had already been a prolonged and arduous struggle.

CHAPTER 6

The Hero Complex

After several weeks at Base Camp, the effects of acclimatisation were palpable. The relentless altitude headaches had finally dissipated, and our oxygen saturation levels showed marked improvement. Merely a week prior, our pulse oximeter readings had plummeted to alarming lows, with some as low as 65 per cent saturation. For context, at sea level, a healthy blood oxygen level typically exceeds 98%, and anything below 90% warrants immediate medical attention. Yet, amidst the thin air of the mountains, a curious phenomenon unfolds: despite these perilously low oxygen readings, climbers remain conscious and capable of executing physical tasks. This enigma has spurred extensive scientific inquiry, with numerous experiments conducted at high altitudes in pursuit of answers. Unravelling the mystery behind our body's resilience to hypoxia could revolutionise medical understanding, particularly in critical care scenarios such as comatose patients with chronically low oxygen levels.

After completing some initial hikes around the Everest Valley to build our strength, we embarked on a 10km hike to the renowned Rongbuk Monastery. This fascinating monastery, nestled among the rocks and looking up at Everest, is one of the few that survived the widespread destruction of Buddhist cultural heritage during the Chinese occupation in the 1950s. At the monastery, we were shown a small hole carved into the solid rock, which served as a hiding place for monks attempting to evade Chinese soldiers' intent on exterminating them.

We then each, in turn, received a blessing from the high Priest Lama, which is traditional, before attempting Everest on the north side.

Everyone in the team received their blessing, but when it came to me, the Lama started making a big deal, placing his forehead against mine and chanting for what seemed like ages.

I'm not religious or superstitious, but with my current state of mind surrounding the climb still being one of apprehension, I took this as a bad omen.

Over the next few nights, when I was alone in my tent, paranoia would slowly creep into my head. Did he know something? Why had the Lama singled me out? Had he sensed something was going to happen to me?

Upon reflection, I now laugh at how my mind wandered into such crazy thoughts. However, back then, alone in a tent at 2 a.m. in freezing conditions, those fears were all too real. Perhaps he sensed that, high on the mountain, I would soon face a decision that would stay with me forever.

The human body is a vulnerable piece of equipment, requiring careful attention and respect, especially in the extreme environment of high-altitude. Ascending Everest too quickly can lead to severe altitude sickness, manifesting as potentially fatal conditions such as pulmonary oedema, where fluid accumulates in the lungs, or cerebral oedema, where the brain swells with excess fluid. Both are treacherous and swift in their lethality. To grasp the rapid onset of altitude sickness, consider this: if you were suddenly transported from sea level to the summit of Everest, you would likely die within an hour due to the dramatic altitude change. Our bodies are simply not designed to function in the oxygen-starved, rarefied air found at such elevations.

Although the human body is fragile, it is also an incredible piece of equipment. With time and gradual adaptation, it learns to meet the demands you place on it. When approaching Everest with a methodical and gradual strategy, your body begins to acclimatise to the high-altitude environment. By slowly increasing your altitude and following the principle of "climb high, sleep low", you allow your body to adapt. Spending days at higher elevations before descending to lower altitudes to rest enables your body to become stronger and more efficient in low-oxygen conditions, ultimately producing more red blood cells to cope with the reduced oxygen levels.

And that's exactly what you have to do with Everest. Those that try to cheat this process tend to fail or die.

As we departed from base camp, our journey commenced with a series of acclimatisation climbs leading us towards Advanced Base Camp, a gruelling trek spanning 13 miles with an altitude gain of almost 1,400 metres. This arduous ascent catapulted us from the high elevation of 5,000 metres to the thin air of 6,400 metres. The initial leg of this endeavour demanded that we halt overnight at an interim camp, our bodies pleading for respite, before pushing forward to reach Advanced Base Camp the following day, our energy reserves depleted.

The first climb to Advanced Base Camp proved to be a formidable trial, casting doubt upon the aspirations of each member to conquer the towering summit standing at 8,848 metres. As we struggled to reach the modest milestone of 6,400 metres, an unspoken unease permeated our thoughts. However, adhering to the unwritten code within our group, we maintained a facade of resilience, concealing any semblance of vulnerability from one another.

As time moves by on the expedition and you have hiked this section many times, you feel the benefits of acclimatisation become stronger and stronger with each ascent.

While it's true that our physical fitness likely gained some improvement during these treks, it's essential to acknowledge that we were already in relatively good shape upon our arrival. So, the most significant factor contributing to our notable progress over the two-month period, traversing back and forth from Basecamp, was undeniably our bodies' enhanced capacity to adapt to the reduced oxygen levels through acclimatisation.

The acclimatisation process is arguably the most critical factor determining success in summiting Everest. Failure to acclimatise adequately, particularly as you near the summit, can tragically result in death. To gauge our readiness for the climb, we made it a habit of regularly monitoring our oxygen levels and heart rates using finger pulse oximeters.

At high altitudes, the body encounters significant physiological challenges. The heart, in particular, must labour more vigorously to deliver oxygen to vital organs due to the thin air. Failure to acclimatise adequately can push heart rates to perilous levels. During one of our rigorous tests, Marcus registered a resting heart rate of 195 beats per minute, a figure that would prompt immediate medical attention at lower altitudes. The gravity of the situation was apparent in Marcus's expression; any further escalation in his heart rate could precipitate a life-threatening cardiac event, casting doubt on his ability to press forward.

In these challenging situations, one might expect to feel sympathy or concern for a struggling climbing colleague. However, witnessing another climber's difficulties can perversely boost your own confidence. This strange psychology operates on the notion that seeing someone else fail or appear weaker somehow makes you feel stronger and more capable of success. Although it's uncomfortable to admit, this reaction is common. Nevertheless, this mindset is misleading; another person's performance has no bearing on your own potential. Yet, as in many aspects of life, we often interpret others' weaknesses as signs of our own strength and forge ahead with renewed determination.

Nobody wants to be the weakest member of the wolf pack. Yet, that's exactly what we risked becoming. We were a pack of seven strong-willed individuals, each with distinct personalities, thrust into the heart of the wilderness. Our collective aim was survival, but the struggle for dominance was palpable as we navigated the treacherous terrain.

With ample time in the evenings, our conversations spanned a wide array of topics, from favourite foods to movies. Without restrictions, any subject was open for discussion, including debates about which countries should be erased from the world map (as in erasing an entire country). North Korea frequently came up, as did the USA, bizarrely voted for by the Americans in our group due to its foreign policy and overconsumption.

One particularly sensitive topic arose only once: whether we had an obligation or duty to abandon our summit attempt to rescue another climber stranded in the Death Zone. We treaded carefully around this subject, acutely aware that any one of us could end up needing a rescue. Each of us was intensely driven to reach the summit, and we knew what lengths we would go to achieve this goal.

All too often, it's easy to conjure up an imagined sequence of events of what should happen in that life-and-death situation on a mountain.

There is a long-standing belief that mountaineers possess a unique brand of bravery, elevating them to the status of heroes. This narrative has been deeply ingrained in our collective consciousness over the last 100 years, fuelled by tales of explorers achieving superhuman feats. These historic stories have shaped our expectations of what it means to be a mountaineer, leading to swift judgements when modern climbers fail to meet these ideals. However, the reality is that today's typical mountaineer is no different from the average person. They do not possess superhuman powers or extraordinary moral virtue; they are ordinary individuals driven by a passion for the mountains.

Whilst sitting in our cold mess tent at Base Camp trying to kill time, I try to break with the established "hero's narrative" to mountaineering and the decisions we are expected to take. I pose a real-life scenario question to the team in this sensitive dilemma: to save or not to save?

Consider this scenario: You're strolling down your neighbourhood's bustling main street when, out of nowhere, a man stumbles and tumbles into the path of an oncoming bus. In the split second that follows, you find yourself standing mere inches away from him, with the harrowing choice of leaping into the road in order to push him out of harm's way or do nothing. There are several possible outcomes ranging from getting injured, one or both of you dying or the slim possibility of you both surviving. I asked, "What would you do?"

The harsh reality is that most individuals wouldn't instinctively leap in front of a speeding bus, and such a decision to refrain from action is often deemed socially acceptable. There's no societal mandate compelling the average person to display such extreme heroism in dire situations. So why then is there an assumption followed by condemnation if a mountaineer does not fulfil the prescribed heroic act?

After posing the bus scenario, Alex wanted to know about the variables. How fast is the bus going? Do I know the man? How old is he? Is there any traffic coming the other way? My argument is that no two situations in mountaineering are ever the same. Each incident must be assessed and handled based on its own unique circumstances rather than assuming a one-size-fits-all approach. It's crucial to recognise that every scenario in the mountains demands a tailored response, considering the specific merits and challenges it presents.

The history of mountaineering incidents and disasters is fraught with opinion and judgement, often from critics who have never faced the challenges themselves. Many of these commentators fail to consider the reality of what they would actually do in such extreme situations.

The debate among the group became intensely heated. Some argued that we should dive in to save each other no matter the cost, while others were less heroic and more pragmatic. Despite using a bus analogy to frame the dilemma, we couldn't mask our true feelings about whether we would risk our lives for one another. Alex's reluctance to share his stance did nothing to build trust within the team. I, too, was equally ambiguous, using various scenarios to evade a direct answer. In fact, the entire team avoided committing to the idea of saving someone, except for Stephan. He firmly stated he would do whatever it took to rescue a teammate, likely influenced by the death of his friend on Everest the previous year. The rest of the group, other than Marcus, Stephan's climbing partner, looked on enviously. The topic was never discussed again.

To familiarise ourselves with the equipment, we arranged ice climbing practice on the overhanging ice columns of the Rongbuk Glacier, which swept past our advanced base camp. This additional training was crucial for the higher sections of Everest during our summit push. Seizing the opportunity for ice climbing practice, we all eagerly embraced the challenge, viewing it as a chance to prove our mettle within the group.

At the towering 40-metre vertical slab of sheer blue glacial ice near Advanced Base Camp, we rigged a top belay rope, ensuring our safety during practice sessions. Each of us eagerly tackled the ice, driven by a desire to showcase our climbing prowess. As we ascended, a remarkable parallel unfolded: our individual approaches to conquering this icy obstacle mirrored the essence of our everyday personalities.

Max and Maverick, their voices in a constant stream, offered commentary as they ascended, assuming the role of instructors and asserting their perceived superiority. This behaviour echoed their demeanour in camp, where they consistently projected an air of experience, demanding recognition of their authority.

Stephan encountered considerable difficulty, evident in his visible struggle and growing frustration. Each failed attempt at securing his ice axe in the glacial ice slab elicited curses in German, adding to his exasperation. This unintentionally became a source of amusement for the rest of the team, somewhat like Stephan evolving into the expedition's comedic figure at Base Camp. While it provided moments of comedy for the team, it also occasionally came at Stephan's expense.

Seb, our seasoned elder in the realm of climbing, approached each ascent with great consideration, embodying a sense of methodical precision that implied a confidence unburdened by the need to prove oneself. His stature as a doctor commanded profound respect within our group, affording him a position of quiet authority that transcended the petty disputes that frequently arose.

I ascended swiftly when my turn came, driven by a desire to showcase my seasoned expertise. My experience paid off as I reached the summit with remarkable speed, leaving me satisfied with my performance. As I began my descent via abseil, I decided to push the envelope further, executing unnecessary and flashy manoeuvres in an attempt to impress. Regrettably, my attempt at flair backfired when a misstep upon reaching the base sent me tumbling onto my backside, eliciting laughter from my companions. While I outwardly joined in the laughter, inwardly, I seethed with frustration at not being taken seriously. Despite my growth since the early stages of the expedition, where self-doubt clouded my perception of my abilities in comparison to others, I still harboured a deep-seated desire to be recognised as a formidable climber and a true contender. Being the butt of jokes was not part of the plan, serving as a reminder that I still carried lingering insecurities.

Marcus, staying true to his nature, lagged behind as the group ascended the icy slope. This familiar behaviour mirrored his approach in various endeavours, be it in other training climbs or advocating for new ideas; he seemed almost hesitant to draw attention or stir any discord.

Alex attacked the ice with speed as he did on most of his climbs; whilst a bit uncoordinated in parts, his style proved effective as he ascended the ice quickly. Secretly, I was happy with my chosen climbing partner. Glad not to be tied to one of the slower members of the group.

From an outsider's perspective, our two-hour climbing session on the glacial ice leading up to our summit attempt was perhaps the clearest reflection of our current social dynamics and group cohesion. Reflecting on the rigours of an Everest expedition, it's evident that beyond the obvious challenges of climbing and enduring extreme physical conditions, one crucial but often overlooked factor is how you survive within the group. The individuals who attempt to climb Everest are inherently selfish and obsessively driven due to the nature of the challenge. It's no surprise that placing such individuals together in one of the most isolated and remote spots on the planet for an extended period, with the constant threat of death, can lead to breakdowns in group dynamics.

An Everest expedition has much in common with the Television social experiment show "Big Brother". Imagine a scenario where random contestants are placed together in a house and observed over time. Now, replace that cosy house with the formidable slopes of Mount Everest. Here, the stakes are infinitely higher, and the emotional strain is far more intense.

I often described my Everest experience as *"Big Brother in the Death Zone"*. Instead of the confinement of four walls, we found ourselves imprisoned by the vast wilderness of the mountains. Our success or failure would be judged by those back home, with our only hope of escape being to survive the expedition. The isolation, stretched over many months with only our small team for company, tested our characters and fears, often pushing us to our breaking points.

After countless hours together in the high-stakes environment of an Everest expedition, it was perhaps inevitable that our strained emotions would eventually boil over and erupt.

CHAPTER 7

The International Poo Incident

During one of those long days at Base Camp near the end of our expedition, after multiple gruelling ascents and descents from the North Col to Camp 1, we returned to Base Camp to regain our strength. It was then that a peculiar sequence of events began to unfold.

After two and a half months together, our group knew each other intimately, including the quirks that could drive each of us crazy. The relentless stress and tension from such a prolonged period of time, with scarce food, long nights confined in the tent, and almost total isolation, were compounded by the mounting fear and anticipation of the impending summit attempt. In hindsight, it seems inevitable that emotions would reach a breaking point. However, I could never have anticipated the manner in which it happened.

On one of our last afternoons at Base Camp, before starting our ascent for the summit attempt, Max, Alex, and I finished a regular game we called SHIT. Despite its crude name, the game had simple yet challenging rules. Each of us selected a large rock about 20 metres away and took turns throwing small stones at it. The goal was to hit the rock four times, one for each letter of the word SHIT. The first two to succeed were safe, but the last man to hit the rock four times was the loser. His punishment was to stand 10 metres away, drop his trousers and underwear, bend over, and expose his bare backside. The two winners then took turns throwing four stones each, aiming to hit the target's exposed rear, trying to lodge a stone in-between his exposed cheeks.

The outcome of this game hinges on several crucial factors. Firstly, your proficiency in ball sports, cultivated through your upbringing, dictates your precision when launching a stone projectile. However, the true test of character lies in whether you find yourself among the victors. The responsibility rests solely on your shoulders as you select the size of the stone and determine the force with which you hurl it at your vulnerable teammate.

The contrast in our abilities became apparent during a game with Max and Alex. Hailing from the States, Max, a seasoned American, showcased impressive throwing skills with remarkable accuracy, traits likely honed through his baseball upbringing. My own proficiency, nurtured by years of playing various ball sports during my youth, was evident. Regrettably, Alex seemed to lack the physical education opportunities afforded to us. His performance in throwing was less than stellar. However, he compensated with adeptness in receiving, a skill highlighted when Max's precisely launched projectile found its mark squarely in Alex's behind.

While the game of SHIT may sound crude, it served as a revealing gauge of the mood and tensions within the team's camp. High tensions or interpersonal conflicts often manifested in the forcefulness with which stones were thrown, allowing for a release of pent-up aggression. Conversely, during times of camaraderie, following an enjoyable movie night and a departure from monotonous meals like eggs, the selection of smaller stones with reduced impact became more common. This shift in stone size not only reflected the camp's mood but also indicated a decreased intent to cause harm, with a greater likelihood of missing the target altogether.

In Base Camp, the game served as a vital source of entertainment during the long stretches of downtime. However, as we neared the end of the day, with anticipation building for our summit weather reports, even this welcomed distraction couldn't alleviate the palpable tension and pervasive boredom that had settled over the camp.

The day began with my reluctance to join Max for our morning yoga session. Instead, I found myself lingering in the familiarity of our cramped tents. These homes, while humble in size, had morphed into our sanctuaries amidst the unforgiving terrain. Each of us had personalised our tents with rugs and carefully organised compartments for our belongings. Despite their modest dimensions, these tents symbolised a sense of belonging and security amidst the harsh reality of our surroundings. Nights plummeted to bone-chilling temperatures of -30 degrees Celsius, often forming icy crusts within our makeshift abodes. Yet, they remained our cherished homes, offering solace amidst the brutal wilderness.

While securing my clothes to the line extending from my tent to Maverick's, I couldn't help but acknowledge its dual role.

Beyond just drying garments, it provided an additional layer of defence, crucial for anchoring our tents against the relentless assault of high winds.

Despite grappling with the challenges of altitude sickness and the unsettling effects of Diamox tablets, which often left our stomachs in turmoil, we frequently endured uncomfortable episodes of loose bowels. Our clothing bore the unfortunate consequences, becoming unwitting casualties of these incidents. Following a personal mishap earlier that day, I seized an opportunity to inject some fun into our tense environment by hanging my soiled pants on Maverick's washing line near his tent. Amidst the mounting tension of our final days, I hoped for a light-hearted reaction to break the monotony. However, tensions had been simmering among us, particularly between myself and the American climbers, Max and Maverick. They misinterpreted my playful gesture as an attempt to assert dominance or provoke conflict, whereas my intention was simply to inject a moment of amusement into our arduous journey. Regrettably, they failed to appreciate the spirit of camaraderie, and they took the game of SHIT with a level of seriousness that I hadn't anticipated.

So, when Maverick came out of his tent and saw my heavily stained pants, he did not take it very well. I started giggling, which I'm sure only enraged him further.

Maverick looked at me with a serious expression and with a strong American accent and said, "Oh, it's like that is it."

After reclaiming my pants, I retreated into the sanctuary of my tent, relishing a moment of respite. As I reclined, thoughts of the formidable summit loomed large once more, reminding me of the monumental challenge that lay ahead.

Approximately 30 minutes later, the zip on my tent opened. Maverick popped his head through and said, "Here you go," he then proceeded to dangle in front of me a small clear plastic bag.

I recoiled backwards in horror into the corner of my tent when I realised what was in the bag. Maverick had in his hand a small transparent bag containing a massive poo floating in urine. Maverick was hovering it over my sleeping bag and all my clothes. If the contents opened in the tent, this could be a real disaster. I kept saying, "Maverick, no, no, don't do it." Ignoring my pleas, Maverick threw the bag into the corner of my tent and left. I lunged to grab it before too much leaked out. Crawling out of my tent, I instinctively launched the bag into the air, aiming to get it as far away as possible. That day, I learned I'm much better at throwing stones than bags of poo.

The bag went high into the air, and I watched almost in slow motion as it covered about 10 metres only to come down onto Dutch Bas's tent.

It was pretty much an explosion, not too dissimilar to a balloon-filled water bomb exploding, however, with a much nastier package.

Faeces and urine covered the exterior and seeped into the front interior of Bas's tent through the open zipper. I vividly recall the moment Bas emerged to investigate the commotion and identify what had struck his tent. As he crawled out, the realisation hit him too late; the stench clued him in just as his hand landed squarely in the mess.

I did what you would expect any normal person to do and

ran away really quickly like a scared schoolboy, knowing he was in trouble.

I soon realised that I had to confront the situation head-on, so I returned to the scene. The entire international team was there, their voices a chaotic mix of German, Dutch, English, Irish, and American accents, all clashing in confusion and anger. The tension was palpable. After months of gruelling mountain living, we were all exhausted, and this incident was the final spark that ignited the explosion. Everyone was blaming everyone. I quietly and sheepishly started saying, "I think I threw it." They stopped and stared. I continued with, "I didn't mean for it to hit your tent, though." As much as I thought this was an explanation, it did not go anywhere to explain why on Earth I was throwing a bag of poo around camp in the first place.

I tried to lighten the mood with a joke, suggesting the mess had come from Maverick's bum. Instead of easing the tension, this joke enraged Maverick, and a full-blown argument erupted once more. Maverick adamantly denied any responsibility. I offered to help clean Bas's tent but insisted Maverick should assist since the mess was his. Maverick refused, leading to another round of heated arguments. My main point was that it would be easier for Maverick to clean up his own mess rather than someone else's. This only sparked further disagreement.

However, within the hour, most of the team had chipped in to help clean up.

The curious aspect of this incident lay not only in its severity but also in its aftermath. Despite the gravity of the situation and its rapid escalation, by the time dinner arrived that evening, and after cleansing our hands of the day's toil, an unexpected camaraderie had emerged. We found ourselves exchanging jokes and sharing laughter as if transported back to a time untouched by the day's events. Though unconventional, this peculiar method of group reconciliation proved remarkably effective in diffusing the palpable tension that had gripped our team, allowing us to realign our focus on our shared objective once more.

The night brought with it the sobering arrival of our initial summit weather report. As the excitement of our journey so far faded into the cold reality of our impending challenge, the gravity of our situation became very real. We were about to confront an unforgiving world that would push us beyond our limits. The playfulness of our earlier days gave way to a sombre acknowledgement of the risks ahead. We understood all too well that not every member of the expedition teams here at Base Camp would return from the summit alive.

CHAPTER 8

It's Out of your Hands

One of Everest's most formidable challenges lies in the absolute dominance of weather over your entire summit attempt. Amid discussions about overcrowding and "traffic jams" on Everest, a critical aspect often gets overlooked: the Himalayan weather at such extreme altitudes affords only a tiny window of opportunity throughout the year.

In the middle of May, a time frame etched in the annals of Everest history, the mountain's weather patterns unfold predictably. For decades, climbers have charted their summit bids to coincide with this narrow window spanning approximately a 2–3-week period. The scientific explanation lies in the seasonal migration of the Indian monsoon, which, upon its arrival in Nepal, exerts its influence on the formidable jet stream winds encircling Everest's summit. This meteorological dance offers a fleeting opportunity for climbers, shielding them from the ferocious gusts that can reach speeds of up to 100 miles per hour, a force capable of sweeping even the most seasoned mountaineers off their precarious perch.

In the world of mountaineering, predicting the ideal window for the four-day summit push becomes a crucial task, transforming everyone into amateur meteorologists. Timing is everything; light winds and favourable weather conditions are paramount for a successful ascent to the Summit. With only one shot at the summit bid, climbers must carefully plan their endeavour, as they possess limited oxygen and personal physical reserves for a single attempt. Misjudgement can have severe consequences; strong winds can force you back or, worse, blow you off. Each year, numerous expeditions fail due to this single factor, leaving behind shattered dreams and disappointed climbers grappling with events seemingly beyond their control.

Mountaineers diligently seek vital information from other expedition teams regarding their planned ascent dates and the rationale behind their decisions. Despite the expectation of open communication, the reality is quite different; crucial weather data is often closely guarded. This secrecy stems from the practical concern of avoiding overcrowding on the route. Revealing precise ascent plans risks creating bottlenecks, potentially endangering climbers and impeding progress.

It can take just a few climbers to block the whole climbing route. If someone gets stuck or has a problem, this then causes time delays for those below, potentially spelling the end to any summit bid.

In the collaborative spirit of mountaineering, there are occasional attempts to organise summit teams in order to establish some semblance of order. These discussions, however, often escalate into heated debates, as each team is determined not to be relegated to a trailing position. During one such intense discussion at base camp, tensions reached a breaking point, resulting in a physical altercation between two separate Sherpa teams, each vying for preferable climbing slots. Amidst the chaos of pushing and shoving, and one individual even resorting to a headlock, the altercation eventually dissipated without resolution. In the end, it was unanimously agreed that teams would climb according to their own schedules. The drive for success on Everest is not exclusive to Western climbers; the livelihood and reputation of Sherpas are equally dependent on our collective success.

Each expedition team relies on weather readings to plan their ascent. While some expensive outfits receive weather predictions from meteorologists abroad, particularly in Europe, the reliability varies. However, when a promising weather report arrives, it sets the entire team on edge, poised for their chance to make a move. They can't afford to hesitate, fearing that a sudden change could jeopardise their expedition before they even attempt the summit.

During my interaction with the disheartened French team on the north side that year, it became evident that the leader's decision to forgo the initial weather window had significant repercussions. Unfortunately, the subsequent summit opportunity didn't arise until a full week later. The leader's confidence in the expected climbing dates led to insufficient planning for his group's Chinese expedition visa. This oversight, compounded by the unpredictable weather, forced the entire French Expedition team to abort their summit attempt, dismantle their camp, and reluctantly depart rather than risk facing legal consequences, including potential imprisonment in a Chinese jail cell for overstaying their visa.

So, after two and a half months of waiting, training and acclimatising when a good weather report comes in, you will definitely go for it.

On the north side, there may be around 200 climbers attempting the ascent over the next three days, which, in reality, constitutes a relatively small number. By comparison, Mount Fuji, at its peak, can host up to 5,000 climbers in a single day. Delays are indeed possible, often caused by just one climber obstructing the route. Media coverage of these "Everest traffic jams" appears somewhat exaggerated. Everest is no longer the exclusive domain of a select few intrepid climbers, largely due to the rise in commercial expeditions. However, despite its allure, the number of climbers remains comparatively low. To put it into perspective, the total number of climbers on Everest over a decade is fewer than those who ascend Snowdon in Wales on a typical summer day.

Choosing the optimal summit day based on accurate weather reports is paramount. I vividly recall encountering an American climber as I descended who had opted to push for the summit a day after my own attempt. Unfortunately, he was caught in a ferocious storm, compelling him to make the difficult decision to retreat.

He pleaded with the rest of his expedition team to make another ascent, but the harsh reality was clear: they lacked the necessary equipment and energy reserves for another attempt. With no other choice, he reluctantly accepted that his summit bid had come to an end, leaving him financially depleted and emotionally defeated. Reluctantly, he began the arduous journey back home, carrying with him the weight of unfulfilled dreams and the bitter taste of failure.

The unpredictable nature of weather, coupled with an array

of potential mishaps, underscores the harsh reality of an Everest expedition: control over outcomes is minimal. From commonplace ailments like the common cold or a bad stomach to more serious setbacks such as twisting an ankle, equipment failures, or even the unexpected closure of climbing routes by the Chinese Government, the list of potential challenges is extensive. In this high-stakes environment, merely possessing physical fitness, strength, and climbing expertise is hardly sufficient. Much of the expedition's success lies beyond one's control. Despite the best preparations, many climbers find themselves drawn back year after year, driven by an unyielding determination to conquer a mountain that consistently eludes them, fuelling an obsession that defies reason.

I mention this primarily to frame our mental state at Base Camp as we awaited our summit weather window. Tension pervaded the atmosphere after enduring months of preparation, leaving us feeling somewhat helpless and entirely subject to the unpredictable whims of the weather.

You could feel the tension in the air, almost anticipating the starter pistol being fired before we could release ourselves on the mountain.

Then, when I almost believed it would never happen, Bas walked into our small mess tent. Sitting there on our little stools, staring up in anticipation, he cracked a little smile and said in his laid-back, Dutch accent, "Hey guys, we're on."

CHAPTER 9

Summit Push

As I hastily start packing my summit bag, I'm overwhelmed with indecision about what to take. After waiting for this moment for over two months and planning the essentials I would need high on the summit, I suddenly feel uncertain. The stark reality of the situation provokes fear within me, leading me to fill my bag with unnecessary items of clothing and food, with a mindset of 'just in case.' When I finally hoist the rucksack onto my back, it weighs over 15 kg. I then spend the next hour tearing through the contents, agonising over every item I discard.

My diary, though small, doesn't justify the additional weight. Leaving it behind at base camp, I'm acutely aware that whatever I write now could be my last words. I don't want negative thoughts of death to creep in at this critical moment, but I realise I need to write something to Abi and Sam in case I don't return. It's strange writing a farewell when I'm trying to suppress these primal fears. As I struggle to block these dark thoughts, I end up writing a letter to Sam, now three months old, asking him to look after his mother when he's older. I'm not sure what I was really writing;

maybe influenced by too many movies and following a Hollywood narrative on what you're supposed to say in these moments.

Either way, the moment I zip my Base Camp tent up for the last time, all those thoughts vanish. I turn to face Everest, whose towering presence has been dominating the landscape since my arrival two months ago. It's no longer a distant giant to be feared and admired from afar. Now, I'm not just a spectator gazing up in awe and trepidation. Now, I must climb it and complete the obsession that began all those years ago.

As I navigate the scree and rock underfoot, my winding path leads me up the Rongbuk Glacier. It's easy to become disoriented in this labyrinth of rock and snow, but every now and then, I catch a glimpse of the deep, blue-green ice of the 10,000-year-old glacier beneath me. Approaching Advanced Base Camp, the glacier, no longer able to contain itself, bursts forth from the ground with 50-metre-high towers of ice. Some of these icy giants are so clear they resemble two-metre-thick sheets of glass, distorting the majestic mountain scenery behind them.

Sometimes, you follow the ice maze to a dead end. Cornered by an ice wall, you retrace your steps, always mindful that you don't walk straight into a crevasse. It's best not to think about what would happen if you plummeted into its depths. The certainty of a dark, cold, lonely death at the bottom, perhaps 200 ft below, just sends a message to your brain of "Beware at all costs."

Having traversed this route three times before during the extensive two-month acclimatisation process, I was fairly familiar with it by now. Despite a few wrong turns, after a long day of trekking, I finally reached Advanced Base Camp. Now focused on my mission, I refuelled, consuming as many calories as possible. I knew that as I ascended, my body's ability to digest food would diminish. As the sun set, I crawled into my tent, acutely aware that the real climb would begin the next day.

By the crack of dawn, I've already completed the short hike to Crampon Point, the official start of the climb where all mountaineering gear must be worn. From this point onward, the mountain reveals why it took pioneers so many years to conquer its lofty summit. Steep ice and rock walls rise vertically for thousands of metres, a formidable challenge to even the most experienced climbers.

Dressed in my one-piece green down suit, I resemble a mountaineering version of an infant in a warm baby grow. I lace up my Olympus Mons boots, named after the tallest mountain on Mars, which is three times the height of Everest. These bright yellow, knee-high boots, resembling moon boots, were my priciest investment at over £750. I bought them with the hope that they'd keep my feet warm and protect me from frostbite.

Secured to my boots are lightweight 12-point crampons, their razor-like steel spikes designed for icy terrain. My harness holds various carabiners and a jumar, essential for attaching to fixed ropes and preventing falls. My camping gear includes everything from sleeping bag to food supplies, but most crucially, my ice axe. This mid-sized, black and red tool is two feet long with a sharp, heavy pick end. I chose it for its robust steel weight, which provides the necessary strength and power to penetrate deep into the ice.

Dressed and ready for action, I approach the first major challenge of the mountain: the North Col. This section, best described as a 500-metre wall of ice and snow, marks the initial true test of the climb. For many, this is where their Everest dream ends, as the sheer steepness and treacherous conditions of the ice wall starkly reveal the harsh realities and immense difficulties of summiting this peak.

Fortunately, over the last two months, I have climbed this section three times, gaining confidence with each ascent on its icy twists and turns.

This time, however, was different. Most of the teams had received the same weather report as us and were on the same summit schedule. There were around 80 climbers, which was enough to create a bottleneck towards the top section near Camp 1. The expedition teams proceeded to slowly take turns tiptoeing over a 30-foot aluminium ladder spanning a crevasse.

Despite having spoken to other expeditions over the past two months, our groups remained largely insular, spread out across the Base Camp plateau. Strangely, this steep, inhospitable vertical ice section became a social meeting point for climbers as we waited in line for a few minutes.

With climbers from various nationalities, I engaged in seemingly ordinary conversations with strangers to pass the time while clinging to the ice at 7,000 metres above sea level. The overriding theme in these interactions was a shared determination to complete the climb. A palpable sense of pressure was building within everyone to keep moving and finish this arduous endeavour.

Just before the ladder crevasse section, I saw Jack from the other expedition team, whom I had befriended at Base Camp over the past few weeks. Too tired to speak, I gave him a friendly poke with my ice axe in the back. We exchanged a glance and a weary smile, wordlessly expressing our mutual relief and excitement to be on this final push at last.

Upon reaching the top of the North Col at Camp 1, Alex and I immediately set about pitching our tent. With light winds and a clear twilight sky, the physical effort of establishing camp went smoothly. At last, I felt acclimatised to the altitude, and my body responded well. Despite blisters and a few sores, the months of preparation were paying off.

The tensions within our team, whether perceived or real, continued to fester. Maverick and Max, sharing a tent, invited Stephan and Marcus over to play Angry Birds on their small computer game. Alex and I, in our tent, were left out. Their laughter, loud and exaggerated, seemed designed to taunt us. Unable to escape the sound, Alex and I lay there, growing more irritated by the minute. I whispered to Alex that they were doing it on purpose, trying to provoke us. My mind churned with the thought that Maverick and Max were deliberately trying to make us jealous. I then overheard Bas being invited to pop his head in to have a quick game, but not me or Alex.

We were trapped in our tents thousands of metres up, unable to move; paranoia took hold. It felt like high-altitude psychosis, similar to the tales of submariners isolated and confined deep underwater, their minds spiralling into suspicion and conspiracy.

Driven by what seemed like a perfectly reasonable response to my perceived threat, I decided later to pee closer to their tent. My vengeful plan was that they might accidentally collect the yellow snow in the dark and melt it for drinking water.

Looking back, I can only laugh in disbelief at what I was thinking and the pressures this expedition had really started to take on me both physically and mentally.

As the first rays of dawn penetrate our tent, I'm already awake and eager to start the day. Today's goal is Camp Two, situated at a gruelling 7,800 metres. The ascent is a monotonous eight-hour grind up an interminable, steep snow ridge, requiring little in the way of technical skill but demanding relentless endurance.

Five hours into the climb, a sharp pain pierces my lungs from the exertion, but I'm hesitant to use my limited supply of oxygen. The three bottles I carry are my lifeline for the higher, more perilous altitudes. Despite the lack of distinctive features in this section, I find a rhythm in the methodical plod, inching my way steadily up the mountain.

A strange sensation begins in the corner of my right eye, starting as a mild annoyance. Gradually, the irritation intensifies, forcing me to blink repeatedly in a futile attempt to alleviate the growing discomfort.

By the time I arrive at Camp Two, I'm in agony. My right eye has developed a burning sensation, feeling like it's on fire. I have no idea what's causing it. As I remove my glacier glasses, I can barely open the eye. Alex looks at me, and from what I can see with my impaired vision, his reaction is one of shock. He pulls back at the sight of my red, swollen eyeball. When I inspect my glacier glasses, the answer becomes clear: the right plastic side is broken and missing. A wave of fear hits me as I realise that I am snow blind.

Contrary to popular belief, snow blindness isn't caused by a blizzard. It's the result of the sun's intensified rays at high altitude, reflected off the brilliant white snow. Without the full protection of glacier glasses, including their enclosed sides, the sun's intensified power slowly and painfully destroys the eye.

I struggle to get the tent up with Alex, cursing myself for being so complacent and allowing myself to get injured in what seemed such an avoidable mistake.

As I lie in my tent, I gingerly press a sock filled with ice against my throbbing eye, surrendering to the discomfort. Helpless and consumed by self-pity, I grapple with the harsh reality that my ascent hangs in the balance. With each passing moment, the swelling persists, and the prospect of reaching the summit dwindles. Throughout the night, a relentless burning sensation torments my senses, a grim reminder of the fragility of my endeavour. In the solitude of my tent, sleep eludes me as I come to terms with the stark truth that a single fracture in my sunglasses threatens to derail my summit bid.

As the sun breaks over the jagged peaks, casting a faint glow on my precarious perch, the anger that fuelled my frustration disappears, leaving behind a resigned acceptance. Through the haze of pain, I cautiously open my right eye, peering out at the dawn's tentative light filtering through the tent fabric. A glimmer of hope emerges as I catch sight of the vibrant orange hue of my sleeping bag. I can see, although dimly. Though still tender and swollen, my eye has regained some semblance of function overnight. With renewed determination, I reach for my other spare goggles, grateful for the protection they now offer. Originally reserved for higher altitudes, they now serve as a shield for my compromised vision, allowing me further passage up the mountain.

As I pack up to leave Camp 2, leaving the tent in place for my return, I have a renewed sense of energy, almost like I have been given a second chance.

I start to climb again; I think to myself that I never want another long sleepless night like that. Unbeknown to me then, Camp Two would again have another night of surprises in store for me.

CHAPTER 10

Highest Camp Site in the World

The terrain beneath me grows increasingly steep, a challenging blend of rock, ice, and snow. Each step demands careful consideration of where I plant my crampons to avoid any potential slips. Despite the fatigue weighing heavily from a sleepless night back at Camp 2, I press on, heartened by the steady progress I'm making and the reassuring functionality of my weaker eye.

Halting to catch my breath, I pause, surveying the landscape before me. Surprisingly, I've yet to tap into my oxygen supply, a decision driven by the lingering worry of depleting it prematurely, particularly as I ascend to higher altitudes where its necessity becomes paramount. Reflecting on my gear choices, I begin to entertain doubts about my frugality, wondering if investing more in additional oxygen canisters would have been a prudent decision. It occurred to me that my relentless penny-pinching, as evidenced by my order of only three bottles, was perhaps misguided.

From my vantage point, I'm afforded a sweeping view of the

Himalayas stretching out in a rugged, unforgiving line to the east.

With each breath, a gnawing sense of dissatisfaction tugs at my core, a subtle reminder that all is not well. The air, thin and reluctant, fails to gratify my lungs as it once did. It's a stark revelation, a sudden awakening to the altitude's unforgiving reality. At over 8,000 metres, I've breached the threshold into Everest's notorious Death Zone, a merciless realm where oxygen levels plummet to a mere 34% of what one finds at sea level. Here, survival hangs by a thread, a precarious balance between life and death. Acclimatisation is a futile hope in this realm; the body, already in a state of slow decay, wages a silent war for existence. Vital functions falter, sacrificed to preserve what little oxygen courses through the bloodstream. Digestion grinds to a halt, a non-essential luxury in the battle for oxygen-starved vital organs. It's a brutal countdown, a relentless march towards inevitable demise, with time as our prime adversary.

Yet, in this realm of uncertainty, death plays no favourites. Each step, each breath, is a gamble with fate. For some, the veil between life and death is thin, a mere whisper in the wind. For others, it stretches into days of agonising anticipation. But make no mistake, the Death Zone's grasp is unyielding, its hunger insatiable. In the end, it claims all, a sombre testament to the harsh realities of high-altitude mountaineering.

After 7 hours, I arrive at Camp 3 at 8,300 metres, by far the highest established camp in the world. The ground is steep with mixed snow and rock, giving the impression that it's impossible to pitch a tent.

Exhausted, I scan my surroundings and notice other expedition groups arriving in similar states of fatigue. They immediately retreat into their pre-pitched tents, greeted by steaming mugs of tea prepared by their Sherpas. As I begin the gruelling task of digging a level platform in the snow with the shovel end of my ice axe, I can't help but resent the wealthy Westerners who enjoy such luxuries. They relax and recuperate while their Sherpas shoulder the burden of the work.

Despite my resentment, I know it's only coming from a place of jealousy, as at this moment, I would happily pay anything to have my tent put up and water melted for me.

With our team's reduced Everest budget, we still managed to get the help of some Sherpas for the final summit attempt. Albeit in line with our minimal budget, as a team, we shared three of these skilled climbers among the seven of us. Despite their small number, the Sherpas proved invaluable when it came to assisting in building the tent platforms from snow and rock dug from the sheer slopes.

Pitching a tent in this extreme environment feels like an eternity. What might be a simple task at lower altitudes becomes a monumental physical endeavour up here. However, our expedition team works together, with everyone pitching in to get the job done. The plan is to set up three tents and squeeze, including the Sherpas, three or four people into each. Fortunately, we only need to endure this arrangement for a few hours, as our summit push is scheduled for around 10 p.m. that evening.

I see Jack with his team standing about 20 metres away whilst multiple Sherpas put a tent up for him in record time. Jack is just sitting with his ice axe planted deep in the ice, securing his position. I am thinking lucky bastard with having all that help. I give him a casual salute to acknowledge him, to which he responds in kind, but I can't help but notice that he looks really nervous. Avoiding my gaze and turning away.

As the first of our tents goes up, Marcus and Stephan dive inside, leaving me, Alex, Max, Maverick, and Bas to set up the remaining ones. While I try to project a sense of teamwork, I'm really eager to claim the next available tent, and I suspect everyone else feels the same. This leads to a peculiar kind of collaboration where we work together to erect a tent, all the while subtly trying to stake our own claims. At this altitude, these silent power plays manifest in small acts: I casually drop my rucksack at the tent's entrance and continue working on the front ice pegs, then I toss a few personal items, like my gloves, inside the tent to mark it as mine. Though unspoken, everyone knows exactly what I'm doing, especially since Stephan and Marcus just did the same. Alex seems willing to accept my selfish manoeuvre, and soon enough, we're inside the tent, grateful for the thin canvas barrier that offers a semblance of security, blocking out the precarious reality of our position.

As I lay there, struggling to breathe and recover, I could hear Max, Maverick and Bas cursing us under their breath as they wrestled with the last of the three tents unaided. Their frustration is justified. Up here, everything feels primal. It's no longer about the challenge of climbing a mountain; it's about survival. This fear has ignited a selfish instinct in me, one that will stay with me as we continue our ascent.

CHAPTER 11

Into the Death Zone

The anticipation is the hardest part. Lying in our tent at 8,300 metres, the pressure builds relentlessly as I contemplate the coming hours. Alex, Tenzing Sherpa, and I are crammed into a two-man tent, each of us clutching a two-foot-long oxygen bottle on our bellies like a lifeline. I feel like a sardine in a can, every movement constrained. As the hours tick by, I know I should try to rest before our 10:50 p.m. departure, but it's impossible. Squeezed between my tent mates, my mind is a whirlwind of fear and anticipation of what the night will bring.

I can hear the crunching of snow underfoot and the fidgeting of other climbers in their nearby tents, who, I can only imagine, are equally gripped by fear. The murmur of expedition teams moving about reaches my ears, their conversations punctuated by gasping breaths. I recognise my friend Jacks distinctively strong Scottish accent as he chats with his teammates. The Swiss team has just arrived in camp, adding to the sense of unease. Suddenly, the harsh reality of our situation hits me: not everyone here, in this small campsite perched high in the Death Zone, will survive this ordeal. The statistics are stark and unforgiving; one of us will not make it through tonight. I force myself into a state of denial, clinging to the hope that it won't be me.

As the hours pass, unable to move in the darkness, my insomnia takes me on a rollercoaster ride through every possible outcome. Mentally exhausted, I'm suddenly startled by my watch's alarm, snapping me out of my daydream. It's just past 10:20 p.m., almost time for the final push. Lying there, squished in my tent, every instinct tells me not to step into the cold night. I know this feeling all too well; it's the same one I get every summit night on all my expeditions. Every rational bone in my body urges me to stay in the relative safety of my warm sleeping bag, avoiding the cold, dark unknown. Secretly, I listen for high winds, hoping they will take the decision out of my hands and allow me to remain in the comfort of the tent. I've learned to be wary of these voices in my head. But then, with the flash of the first head torch being switched on, the dark spell of fear is broken, and my focus returns.

In the cramped tent, we take turns preparing our equipment. There's not much to put on besides our boots and harnesses, as we've stayed fully dressed in our down suits. Despite this, it still takes the three of us 30 minutes of clambering over each other to be fully kitted and ready to step outside.

Feeling pleased with myself, I surveyed the campsite. Jack and his expedition team had already departed, leaving his tent's zip open, a clear sign of their hasty departure. To my right, I noticed Marcus, Stephan, Seb, Maverick, Max, and Bas were still in their tents. Their tents, positioned about ten metres away, were dark and silent. Not a single light flickered inside them. I march over to one of their tents, suddenly catching my breath, almost forgetting where I am. I call out, "Time to get up, boys; you're late." I don't hear a reply. With no noise or lights coming from their tents, I unzip one and shine the light of my head torch inside. Expecting to see my team packed like sardines in their sleeping bags, I'm bewildered to find the tent empty. Climbing over to the other tent, I peer inside only to be met with the same eerie sight: empty sleeping bags with no sign of my expedition team.

As I walk slowly back to Alex, my mind, starved for oxygen, struggles to comprehend the situation. A Sherpa from another expedition approaches, delivering the unwelcome news: my team has already embarked on the summit push due to growing cold and impatience, departing at 10:15 p.m. It suddenly dawns on me: I've misheard the departure time as 10:50 p.m., a critical misunderstanding that throws our plans into disarray. I recall my initial hesitation at the oddity of the timing, but I brushed it aside. Yet, this seemingly trivial error now places our summit attempt at a disadvantage before it even begins. We find ourselves not only behind schedule but also isolated from the rest of our expedition companions. Frustration and self-directed curses consume me for a brief moment before urgency takes hold. It feels as though the mountain is slipping through my fingers, prompting a fierce determination to regain lost ground.

I push forward with reckless speed, a pace I know deep down is unsustainable. Barely out of Camp 3, I drive my ice axe into the icy surface as I ascend a steep gully. The darkness envelopes me, transforming my world into a narrow tunnel illuminated only by the narrow beam of my headtorch. It's disorienting and easy to lose sight of reality amidst the shadows. Despite my urgency to regain lost time, I'm forced to confront the consequences of my haste. Each step drains precious oxygen, and each exertion adds to my growing fatigue. I can sense Alex struggling to keep up, the strain is evident in his lagging pace.

Then, a sudden, searing pain rips through my chest as I reach upward to secure my next hold. I'm immobilised, stunned by the intensity of the injury, a torn chest muscle from overexertion. I anchor my crampons into the ice, grappling with the pain like a wounded animal. As I catch my breath, my gaze falls on a dark figure mere metres away. With a trembling hand, I direct my headtorch towards the form, revealing the frozen face of a long-deceased climber. I avert my eyes, but the image haunts me as I force myself to press onward, denying the fear that gnaws at the edges of my consciousness. I fix my gaze upward, refusing to acknowledge the precipitous drop below.

As my pace slackens, Alex draws level with me once more. No words pass between us, no acknowledgement of the fallen climber below, just a silent understanding that we're reunited and pressing onward, ever upward. Soon, we will overtake Stephan and Marcus. It's not a competition, but there's a sense of reassurance in our progress. In the darkness, with no visible landmarks, success on the mountain is measured largely by comparison to others. Though not a foolproof gauge, overtaking our fellow climbers reaffirms that I've made up for lost time. Passing Stephan on a treacherous stretch of ice, we exchange a thumbs-up, a silent affirmation of solidarity amidst the concealed expressions of fear and exhaustion behind our oxygen masks and goggles.

As I climb higher and higher into the night, my mind switches to its next major obstacle, the infamous challenge of the Second Step.

Perched high in the perilous Death Zone on Everest's north side, the Second Step stands as the pinnacle of technical challenge on the ascent. A sheer, 100-foot cliff of vertical rock guards passage to the summit, marking the disputed terrain that once challenged the legendary Mallory and Irvine. The abrupt transition from snow and ice to exposed rock presents a formidable hurdle, compounded by the inadequacy of equipment designed primarily for icy conditions.

The steel points of my crampons are useless against the unforgiving rock. Instead of securing a foothold, they produce a shrill, high-pitched scrape as they slide ineffectively. My large mitten gloves further hinder my efforts; I fumble awkwardly, unable to grip the small rock holds I need to ascend. Desperation sets in as I remove my mittens, hoping for better control. The relief is short-lived. The minus 30-degree air immediately assaults my already numb fingers, threatening frostbite. The very gloves designed to protect me from the cold have become my enemy, reducing my attempts at climbing to a futile struggle, like trying to scale a rock face with oven mitts.'

As I clamber over a small rock ledge, I peer tentatively to my right. The moon illuminates a sheer, 2,000-foot abyss below me, its bottom lost in darkness. Deciding its best not to dwell on the seemingly endless drop, I fix my gaze on the cold rock face ahead. Drawing on my rock-climbing experience, I methodically focus on using my legs to bear the brunt of the effort, sparing my arms from premature fatigue. Despite my best efforts to maintain control, I find myself scrambling onto ledges with my knees and belly like a frightened child. It's undignified, but this clumsy, makeshift climbing style seems to be effective.

After 30 minutes of employing unorthodox climbing manoeuvres, I finally conquer the second step. A sense of accomplishment washes over me, but it's swiftly replaced by an unsettling silence. Glancing around, I'm struck by the absence of fellow climbers. Where is Alex? Was I ahead or behind? There's no sight or sound of anyone nearby. Could the altitude be toying with my senses? I've been so consumed by the ascent that I've scarcely entertained any other thoughts.

Standing alone amidst the unforgiving terrain, a chilling realisation grips me: I have no knowledge of the whereabouts of the next oxygen drop to replenish my rapidly dwindling supply. Somewhere amidst the icy expanse atop the treacherous Second Step lies the buried cache, containing what remains of my meagre three bottles. It strikes me with brutal clarity that proceeding without retrieving it would be a fatal mistake; I simply won't have enough oxygen to ensure my survival on the descent. While the understanding that our expedition was unguided had always been known, the stark reality of our situation becomes painfully clear as the night wears on. The ramifications of operating on a tight budget and with limited oxygen reserves begin to manifest themselves with alarming clarity.

Left with no alternative but to perch on a small rock above the second step, I resign myself to waiting, clinging to the faint hope that someone will come. At this moment, the harsh reality of my situation crashes down upon me with brutal force. Alone in the enveloping darkness, stranded without additional oxygen in

Everest's unforgiving Death Zone, the gravity of my predicament sinks in. My summit attempt is over, or worse, I am dead.

At an altitude of over 8,600m, I have nothing to do other than look around, seeing the stars and moon lighting up parts of the mountain. There is no wind, and it feels so still that I can feel my heart beating. "Shit, I fucked it up," I whisper, almost feeling sorry for myself. I curse myself for overlooking such a crucial detail. Without one of the Sherpas, who is still trailing behind somewhere, I'll never locate the hidden oxygen bottle. Glancing at my oxygen gauge, I grimace at the dwindling supply; barely 20% remains. It's a chilling realisation. With such a foolish mistake, it feels as though I've just signed my own death warrant.

I turn my head light off to save the batteries and close the valve on my regulator to preserve the last of my oxygen.

As I sit in the enveloping darkness, a profound sense of isolation settles over me, similar to being marooned on the desolate surface of the moon, surrounded only by distant stars. I attempt to draw comfort from the frigid, solitary expanse, telling myself that I'm accustomed to such extreme environments and that the night is my ally. But deep down, I know it's a facade, a feeble attempt to bolster my faltering confidence. In truth, you never truly acclimate to the darkness, but I don't really want to admit to myself that I am scared.

I've encountered this fear countless times, grappling with the unseen spectres that haunt the darkness. It's a natural response; our minds, unaccustomed to nocturnal surroundings, tend to fabricate monsters to fill the void. When plagued by fear and negativity, the night becomes a canvas for all manner of horrors to materialise before us.

I've encountered numerous challenges throughout my life, each experience adding to my collection. Whether it was tracking murder suspects under cover of darkness during my time in law enforcement, lying in wait during military exercises in the depths of a dense dark forest, or gazing into the murky expanse of the open sea while swimming across the English Channel at night, I've grappled with the primal fear that lurks in the unknown. It's a fear that never quite leaves us, though perhaps we grow more accustomed to its presence over time.

Stuck high on Everest, I find myself wallowing in self-pity, mourning the possibility of never seeing my newborn son again. Desperately, I fight against the tide of negative, ominous thoughts threatening to engulf me. I hold my breath, straining to detect any signs of approaching company. My ears deceive me, teasing with the sound of footsteps that turn out to be nothing more than the wind's playful antics. Anger wells up within me, directed at Alex for delaying Tenzing Sherpa, the key to locating the oxygen drop. Yet, beneath the surface, I know the blame lies squarely on my shoulders; I rushed ahead thoughtlessly, failing to keep track of their progress.

Just as I'm drifting into a cold, hypoxic dream, I hear something, or I think I do. My mind snaps back as I suddenly see lights coming from below.

Though it seems like an eternity, only thirty minutes have passed when Alex's face appears around the corner of the rock ahead. He recounts the obstacle he faced: three Chinese climbers had stalled on the second ladder section, one of them frozen in place, impeding his progress.

We're back in action. Tenzing Sherpa, who had assisted with the oxygen drop a week earlier, leads me to the concealed cache of O2. While there's a standard climbers' etiquette dictating that one shouldn't tamper with another expedition team's oxygen supplies, the reality is often different. In moments of desperation, these vital bottles sometimes vanish. Hence, it's imperative to bury them where only your team knows their whereabouts. Discovering an empty stash at your oxygen checkpoint can prove fatal. Regrettably, incidents of oxygen theft are frequently omitted from Everest narratives, as they don't align with the honourable conduct typically associated with the sport.

I carefully unscrew my regulator and affix it to the new bottle, a task fraught with potential peril. One wrong move, leaving the valve open while attaching it, could render the delicate regulator useless, locking it onto a maximum oxygen flow rate. In such a scenario, my oxygen would deplete in a mere two hours, a virtual death sentence, especially considering this is my last bottle. Mindful of the stakes, I gingerly manoeuvre my bulky mittens, ensuring each twist is deliberate and precise.

This being the last of my three oxygen bottles, I turned the valve onto the lowest flow rate to conserve it.

Amongst the affluent climbers on the mountain, nicknamed "max flow" by our team, there were those who could afford the luxury of setting their regulators to the maximum flow rate across all their oxygen bottles. With eight or more bottles at their disposal, their Sherpas catered to their needs, dispensing oxygen as required. Unfortunately, I was not among the privileged few. At that moment, however, I would have eagerly paid for such an upgrade.

Reunited and replenished with oxygen, we forge ahead, ascending ever higher along Everest's Northeast Ridge. As the climb progresses smoothly, I find myself lulled into a false sense of security, almost dismissing the possibility of any mishaps befalling me. It's a common mindset among climbers to believe that accidents are something that happens to others and not you. Yet it's precisely this complacency that often leads to disaster.

CHAPTER 12

Head First

My pace quickens as I ascend. From my elevated position, I gaze out over the vast expanse of Tibet. The moon casts its beautiful glow upon the seemingly infinite range of snow-capped mountains to the east. It's a rare moment of indulgence, the first time I allow myself to savour the breathtaking view.

I'm climbing higher into the Death Zone, but everything has changed. My mood has lifted, the grip of death has started to loosen, and I can relax a bit. I've got this in the bag.

Amidst the brief respite of relaxation, a momentary lapse in focus leads to a seemingly insignificant error. On a section of the climb that offers a bit of reprieve, I pick up the pace, allowing my thoughts to wander homeward. Images of the Kathmandu Steak House, renowned for its exquisite Calcutta beef, dance through my mind and I laugh to myself. At this point, any semblance of luxury holds appeal. Rumdoodles, another restaurant in Kathmandu, boasts an intriguing offer: free dinners for life for Everest summiteers. The quality of the fare may leave much to be desired, but at this moment, any alternative is preferable to the monotonous diet of eggs that has sustained me for the past two months.

In my dazed state, my mind drifts to thoughts of high-protein steaks, exactly the distraction I had warned myself against. My left foot slips just an inch too far over the ledge, and suddenly, I'm hurtling headfirst down the sheer slopes of the North Face of Everest. A yelp escapes my lips as panic grips me, my hands clawing desperately at the ice in a futile attempt to halt my descent. The ice axe I've relied on feels utterly inadequate as it bounces off the frozen surface with each futile attempt to arrest my fall. Everything blurs into a surreal slow-motion sequence, a grim prelude to what seems like an inevitable plunge to my death.'

In the throes of panic, I barely register what's happening before the rope jerks taut, slamming me forcefully into the unforgiving rock face. The impact jars my face and right shoulder against the jagged surface, tearing my oxygen mask away in the process. I freeze, gasping for air, the taste of metallic blood flooding my mouth. After an agonising few seconds, I realise the fixed-line rope has arrested my fall. Assessing the situation, I realised that one of the anchor points in the ice must have failed, allowing me to fall as far as I did. Despite the heart-stopping drop of approximately 30 ft, I'm filled with a surge of gratitude; the one remaining aluminium anchor spike secured above has held firm, sparing me from a potentially 3,000-foot drop into the abyss below.

For what feels like an eternity, I hang suspended, frozen in terror, my body refusing to budge. Below me lies a sheer drop, a gaping void of uncertainty. I dare not move, unsure of the strength of the lone anchor that holds me in place. Will it hold, or will it give way, plunging me into the abyss of Everest's North Face? The thought gnaws at me, propelling me into action. With a surge of adrenaline, I begin to assess the damage, starting from my feet and working my way up to my pounding head. Despite the numbness creeping into my shoulder and the sting of a battered nose, I repeat to myself: "I'm okay." A mantra in a desperate attempt to convince myself of a truth I'm not entirely sure of.

As the rush of adrenaline fades, my hands tremble, a stark reminder of the perilous situation I find myself in. I cast a wary glance upward, steeling myself for the arduous climb ahead. Each movement is deliberate and methodical, a testament to my determination to avoid further mistakes. The slope looms before me, a daunting 80-degree incline littered with precarious ledges of rock, ice, and snow. With each step, I dig my crampons deep into the hard ice, simultaneously hauling myself upward with the aid of the rope. My mask hangs limply at my side, its absence of supplemental oxygen a harsh reminder of the thin, biting air that fills my lungs.

As I climb, the steel prongs of my crampons scrape against unforgiving rock, an unnerving cacophony of sound that echoes through the desolate landscape. Each narrow ledge offers a brief respite, a fleeting moment of reprieve in the face of overwhelming adversity. I dare not look down; my focus solely fixed on the task at hand: reclaiming the safety of the ice anchor that has spared me from certain doom.

Exhaustion engulfs me, the culmination of a monumental effort draining the last reserves of my energy. I slump against the anchor point, my mind a blank canvas against the breathtaking vista before me. Blood oozes from cracked lips, mingling with the frost on my beard, forming crimson icicles that cling stubbornly to my face. Too weary to wipe them away, they freeze in place, a chilling testament to the harshness of this unforgiving environment.

With trembling hands, I cling to the metal anchor point, seeking solace in its cold embrace. My headtorch casts an eerie glow, illuminating the twenty-inch steel stake that secures my precarious perch. A closer inspection reveals its grim reality: the anchor has become dislodged, its two-inch tip barely clinging to the icy surface. I envision the final ice anchor tearing free, my body crashing thousands of feet into the treacherous glacier below.

Falling off a mountain or a cliff is a constant, looming threat in the mind of every mountaineer. No matter how much you try to suppress this fear, it lingers in the shadows, a relentless reminder of your imminent mortality.

Hollywood has not assisted with this primitive fear and has done some fantastic action shots of mountaineering accidents with highly dramatised scenes of climbers falling to their deaths.

Over the years, after experiencing a few falls myself, I've come to understand the true nature of these moments. There's no time for reflection or recognition; one minute, you're climbing, and the next, you're plummeting. The transition is so sudden and jarring that you barely grasp what's happening. This disorientation is compounded at high altitudes, where your oxygen starved brain processes everything sluggishly, operating at half its normal capacity.

Feeling brave enough to peer over the edge and see where I had just fallen, I noticed some of my climbing gear scattered a few metres below. It must have tumbled out of my bag during the fall. I spotted my spare black hat and my water bottle, with a small amount of frozen water in it. Despite knowing the water was frozen and useless, my hypoxic, oxygen-starved mind was fixated on retrieving it. The high altitude was clearly impairing my judgement, leading to poor decisions. Perhaps my protective instinct stemmed from the hard-earned nature of my kit, but rationalising my actions was nearly impossible in my oxygen-deprived state. Just as I was about to unclip from the rope and descend, a moment of clarity hit me. I started giggling at the absurdity of risking my life for a frozen water bottle.

I fix my oxygen mask back over my mouth and nose, clearing some of the ice blood from my face. I tell myself I have to slow down. I can't make any more mistakes.

As if to drive home this harsh reality, my head torch catches the faded red jacket of a dead, frozen climber just two feet away. The faded red fabric of his one-piece down suit speaks of decades of ultraviolet exposure at his final resting place. I try not to picture his last moments, but I can't help but wonder about the torment he faced.

"Focus, Focus," I keep saying to myself out loud, trying hard to break free from the fear that is gripping me. I feel exhausted and sleepy. Deep down, I know that High Altitude Cerebral Oedema is setting in. My oxygen-deprived brain is being squeezed by the increasing fluid, and I realise that if I stay here too long, my eyes will close, and I will never wake up. I will join this unknown dead climber in his high resting place.

As my mind battles the overwhelming urge to sleep, I begin

to accept the grim reality that this spot high in the Death Zone could be my final resting place. I shake my head, trying to resist this negative mindset, but the exhaustion is pulling me towards sleep. I almost feel ready to surrender, believing I have nothing left. In a desperate attempt to stay conscious, I search my thoughts for a time when it was this bad. I need something to draw on to get through this.

Then suddenly comes a wave of strength as I recall how I had pushed through all those years ago despite the pain.

Three years earlier, on a cold winter's night in the Brecon Beacons of Wales, I faced a similar ordeal. During the final hours of our army endurance exercise, the 70-pound Bergen on my back cut into my shoulders, and I could barely grip my assault rifle with my frozen fingers. Exhausted and lost in the snowstorm, I was at the end of my limits. Somehow, I managed to flick a switch. Though physically and mentally exhausted, I found another gear that allowed my exhausted body to press on. Now, I need to draw on that experience. After all, I've been to this dark place of despair before.

CHAPTER 13

Selection

"Are you a fucking twat?!" screams the Directing Staff, so close up to my face that I can feel bits of his spit land on my lip. It's 4.30 a.m. midwinter somewhere in a remote spot of the Brecon Beacons mountains, Wales. I'm halfway through SAS selection, and our small platoon is called to attention for inspection. I crawl out of my little wet hole, where I've managed to snatch about 20 minutes of sleep. Despite being soaked to the bone, I'm grateful for the brief rest.

While shivering uncontrollably, the Directing Staff (DS) bombards me with insults for not having a small "gash bag" (rubbish bag) for my leftover trash. I attempt to appease him with the plastic wrapper of my boil-in-the-bag meal, but this only fuels his anger further.

Screaming at the top of his voice, he shouts.

"Are you trying to cheat me?"

"Get your fucking arse into those mountains and find me the perfect boulder from the bottom of a river."

Without questioning what was clearly a very bizarre request, I quickly shout, "Yes, staff!" and disappear into the dead of night in the middle of the Beacons on a boulder hunt.

Not being entirely sure what the "perfect boulder" was or exactly why I was being punished, I reconciled myself that one does not exist and it was just another test of hardship to try and get me to withdraw from Selection.

I think about grabbing any old rock and bringing it back but soon realise that I'm probably being followed and that the rock would have to be smooth from being in a river bed anyway.

Twenty minutes later, I found myself waist-deep in freezing water, struggling to lift a 5-kg boulder from the dark, murky depths. I eventually brought it back to the DS, feeling like a loyal dog retrieving a ball, only to discover he had long since left. The remaining Directing Staff stood around, mocking and laughing at me, calling me a twat.

This was one of the many times through physical SAS selection that I thought of quitting. The prospect of a nice, warm bed back home compared to this cold, pointless humiliation was sometimes almost overwhelming.

Physical selection for the Special Air Service (SAS) varies and has changed overtime, but for me, it was a nine-month build-up for the Reserve 21 SAS Regiment, culminating in the notorious Test Week with the regular 22 SAS unit. Just like on Everest, sitting in a freezing tent amidst a gale-force storm in Tibet, I often found myself questioning how I ended up in such extreme situations. The challenges of the SAS were no different

In the middle of winter, on Test Week on the final exercise of Physical Selection, after an arduous week of running around the mountains in the snow, we had the epic Endurance or Long

Drag to complete.

Exhaustion mixed with mild hypothermia is difficult to describe; it feels like being detached from your body. You drift in and out of daydreams, barely aware of your surroundings, until a harsh jolt brings you back as you twist your ankle and buckle under the weight of your Bergen. This 70-kilometre self-navigation march through the Brecon Beacon mountains in a snowstorm on a winter's night, with a 70-pound Bergen on my back and an automatic rifle in hand, made me question how I ended up there.

Stepping into the 21 Special Air Service Barracks for the first time was intimidating. Uncertainty lingered in the air, and I felt a sense of unease. I recall feeling underprepared, almost inadequate, as if my physical strength fell short. I opted to keep my puffer jacket on, even within the hot office, hoping to appear bigger. Yet, this misguided notion couldn't have been further from the truth. In the challenging year that lay ahead, muscle mass held little sway. Instead, we faced weeks of navigating the cold, damp terrain of the Brecon Beacons, sleeping in small holes beneath the trees. This trial was about testing willpower and endurance, qualities I had honed over years spent amidst the mountains. My extensive experience leading expeditions in high-altitude settings, where oxygen levels dwindle to half that of sea level, provided a distinct advantage during the gruelling selection course.

From my squadron, I was one of 30 new intakes, and along with those Squadrons based in London and Scotland SAS Reserve units, we totalled 102 new recruits. The Special Forces selection process over the next year in the winters of the Welsh mountain terrain would test me to my mental and physical core.

Pre-selection comprised a six-month preparation phase before the actual selection commenced. This phase involved regular attendance at the barracks, organising equipment, attending navigation lectures, and engaging in a series of squad training runs in the local terrain. The intensity of these runs progressively increased, with training staff continually pushing us to our limits, effectively weeding out those who were not up to it.

I remember vividly how the directing staff would humiliate and shout at everyone at the end of each session, questioning the purpose of them carrying on if they couldn't even keep pace on what they deemed as an "easy" run. However, as someone who was a keen runner, I knew these runs were far from easy.

Many inquire about the fitness requirements for passing the gruelling SAS selection process, to which I always stress the importance of being a good runner at heart. After all, during test week, you essentially navigate the hills at speed, albeit at a slower pace, due to the burden of carrying a small donkey (bag) on your back. I often suggest that a good benchmark is the ability to run 10 miles in 1 hour on the road without any additional weight.

I understood that the staff's tactics aimed to psych us out. Predictably, these psychological strategies, even in the initial phase, unsettled some newcomers, eroding their confidence until they withdrew.

Forming bonds with a good bunch of guys within the unit, I spent most of my time with them. Just as in selecting a climbing partner on Everest, SAS selection demanded careful choices, knowing well that your survival would depend on it.

Similarly to my approach on Everest, where selecting a climbing partner who could maintain pace was crucial for success, I applied the same principle to Selection. I deliberately opted for individuals who demonstrated not only speed in the running but also exhibited proficiency in weapons training and map reading, recognising their strengths.

During SAS Selection, most had nicknames, and I got along well with Taz. He was a formidable man with a massive build. Taz earned his nickname not only because of his growling voice but also because he resembled the cartoon version of the Tasmanian Devil.

Then there was Rhys. Rhys and I formed a lasting friendship, one that endured through the toughest times. He was a well-rounded individual, easy to get along with, and committed to the long haul. Rhys's resilience allowed him to look beyond any bad day he encountered.

Over the following years, our lives diverged dramatically. Taz pursued a political career, running for election as a UKIP MP. Rhys remained dedicated, continuing his active deployments with the SAS. As for me, I set my sights on Everest.

During the pre-selection process, we were frequently paired with another trooper recruit. On a typical selection weekend, I would drive from Bristol to the barracks in Wales, constantly checking the weather report. The thought of enduring the next few days in freezing, torrential rain filled me with dread.

I often got paired up with Rhys as we were similar in physical ability, but moreover, I was always happy as we got on well and tended to manage to deal with most scenarios that got thrown at us.

On one particularly bad weather weekend in the depths of the

Brecon Beacons, during a fierce winter storm, many of the recruits were scattered across the mountains. They were navigating from one objective to another, which often cruelly meant checkpoints on several different summits. With driving rain and darkness, our map and compass skills had to be spot on.

To progress to the mountain phase of selection, we had to pass a challenging map and compass exam. Nights like this one made it clear why. Visibility was zero, and the rain was freezing cold. Our instructions were clear: if we got lost, we should follow a basic survival procedure. This meant finding a small stream and following it as it grew into a river, which would eventually lead to some form of civilisation. There, we could find a phone box and call a memorised emergency number in Hereford.

On this night, some teams got completely lost and ended up over 30 miles away in random villages, calling in to get rescued.

Rhys and I, after nearly 12 hours out on the hills, were on the brink of collapse and thought this might be the end of our selection. Eventually, we stumbled onto a small road and started walking along it, risking an instant bollocking if seen by the directing staff. Desperation pushed us further; when we saw a vehicle approaching, we jumped into the road and waved it down frantically. The vehicle, an old VW-style camper van, promptly stopped in the middle of the road. In hindsight, I realise they likely stopped because we were waving automatic assault rifles. We fabricated a story about being on exercise, and they let us into the back of the van, where we lay down to avoid being seen. They kept asking what we were doing, clearly aware we were on SAS selection as the area is known for it, but we maintained the pretence of being a standard army unit.

After a short lift, they dropped us just short of the makeshift camp. We marched into the command post five hours overdue, bracing for the worst. Instead, we were greeted with hot tea and congratulations for being the second team back; everyone else was either completely lost or had given up. It was a valuable lesson: not to throw in the towel when things seemed dire and to remember that if we were struggling, chances were everyone else was too.

Having completed the six-month preselection process, we were informed if we had met the standards to attempt the notorious Test Week. This final phase would determine our pass or fail for SAS physical selection.

By the time Test Week arrived, I was prepared. It had been over a year since I signed up with the Regiment, and I felt both fit and strong. I had been trained in the use of various weapons and special forces tactics, feeling ready. Two weeks before Test Week, we were careful to avoid injuries. Instead of running around the mountains, we spent our time familiarising ourselves with different weapons, particularly stripping and reassembling AK47 assault rifles as quickly as possible. To distract ourselves, we engaged in toned-down close-quarter combat training, including knife-fighting drills. Despite our efforts, the impending Test Week loomed like a heavy threat in our minds. We knew that all our hard work was about to culminate in a gruelling test, and we were fully aware of the pain that awaited us.

Test Week in Winter selection is inherently unpredictable due to the weather. During this week-long endurance test, each day would see you driven to a new location in the Brecon Beacons and Elan Valley in Wales. With your heavy Bergen and assault rifle, you would set off individually, equipped with map coordinates, and navigate swiftly to reach each checkpoint. The task is straightforward: meet each point within the required time, traversing up and down the mountains. There are no ifs, no buts, and no excuses; just reach the checkpoints on time or fail.

I remember the first cold start to test week, loaded into the back of an army wagon at 4 a.m. on a pitch-black winter's morning. The directing staff called out our numbers, stripping away our names. Being reduced to a number in the dark, unsure of our destination, was unsettling. Everyone in the back was silent, sharing the same sense of anticipation and fear. It felt very similar to cattle heading to slaughter, unaware of what lay ahead but certain it wouldn't be good.

This sombre mood was only broken by Taz when he spoke out in the dark silence to the directing staff, saying in his thick Welsh-Tasmanian devil accent, "Sorry staff, I've forgotten my number; what was it?" This gave everyone a little chuckle as we were about to be tested on one of the hardest elite military courses in the world, and he could not even remember his two-digit number.

Through all our training, we had become well acquainted with various parts of the Beacons. Although the selection process kept our daily routes a mystery, we had come to understand the terrain deeply. Over the last year and a half, I had spent every spare moment running different paths in these mountains. Some routes had names like Superman, Ironman, Ricochet, or Point to Point, each presenting its own challenges in navigation, distance, and terrain.

As test week began, I pushed myself hard, moving at speed for up to seven hours each day, knowing that every minute counted if I wanted to pass. Each time I reached a checkpoint, I received a new set of coordinates. These were given only once, so I had to memorise the six-digit grid reference quickly. I then plotted it on the map and set a bearing on my compass, all within 15 seconds. Sometimes the directing staff would start asking you stupid questions like, "What's your favourite film?" so as to confuse me a bit. Once I had my new bearing, I knew I had to push forward. With the heavy weight on my back and my weapon in hand, running uphill was a struggle, but it was necessary. Every second was crucial if I wanted to beat the cut-off time.

In normal navigation, you'd typically choose the easiest, most pleasant route. However, during Selection, it was about taking the most direct path and pushing through whatever was in front of you. This approach could sometimes backfire when the ground was too steep or the terrain too boggy, slowing me down. Yet, it still proved the most time-efficient, rather than trying to contour around a mountain or avoid certain features.

Even going to the toilet, I couldn't afford the luxury of a stop. To stay hydrated, I drank plenty of fluids with electrolytes and, although unpleasant, would relieve myself by peeing in my trousers when crossing rivers and letting it wash away. As harsh as it sounds, not stopping saved precious minutes. These saved moments, combined with running hard every second, provided a crucial advantage. The Ministry of Defence had deemed it necessary that for this selection course, for both 21 and 23 regiments, the average overall tabbing speed was to be increased to 4km per hour to match that of the regular 22 SAS unit.

After six days of gruelling hardship during Test Week, we all gathered in the barracks to find out who had passed this phase of selection and who would be permitted to move on to the next phase: Endurance. Endurance, also known as the Long Drag, is the final test where we must cover over 70 kilometres through the Brecon Beacons alone and in under 20 hours.

In a strange, almost perverse way, we hung on the directing staff's every word, hoping we had passed and could face the next stage of pain. Out of the 102 troopers who began this process a year and a half ago, only three of us remained to proceed to the Endurance phase. Sadly, none of my friends made the cut this time round.

We had two hours to gather our things before the three of us were bundled into the back of a van, joining the rest of the 22 SAS for the Long Drag. Our Bergens were added more weight as they were weighed in front of us. Then, one by one, with our weapons in hand, we received our next checkpoint coordinates and were sent off into the dead of night to cover the entire length of the Brecon Beacons.

The weather had turned, and a snowstorm engulfed the mountains in Wales, making the ground difficult to navigate as it transformed into slushy snow. My Bergen pack acted like a sponge, absorbing the melted snow and increasing the weight on my back. Carrying a Bergen is best compared to having a small adult clinging to your back for 20 hours, digging into your shoulders the entire time. After 15 hours, the pack becomes unbearable, and as the hours pass, fatigue sets in. Eventually, its weight begins to feel like a curse.

Not only did we have to traverse the entire length of the Beacons, but we also had to turn around and return via a different route. As darkness fell once more, I entered my second night of the Endurance March, now 17 hours into the test. Reaching the top of the Horse shoe Ridge, which connects to Pen Y Fan, a popular route among hikers, the snow was now deep, almost up to my knees. I had linked up with the two other troopers from 21 SAS, and although running together was technically against the rules, no one was monitoring us in these remote spots.

Looking down the steep, 50-degree slope, we deliberated on our descent strategy. Opting to employ my Bergen as a sledge, with my companions following suit, we descended the 200-metre incline of Pen Y Fan. The delight of speeding down the mountainside momentarily relieved us from the weight of our bags, making us let out playful shouts. However, our excitement was abruptly cut as our exuberant cries led us straight into the next checkpoint. I'm not sure who was more surprised, us at realising we had just found the checkpoint or the directing staff witnessing a bunch of jokers on selection having a sledging session. After being suitably shouted at and reminded that we were meant to be covert elite soldiers, which did not involve screaming in the snow, they sent us on to our final end point.

Honestly, I sensed the exhaustion among the directing staff, too. While they weren't enduring the march themselves, they were forced to endure the wait at the checkpoint for countless hours. Personally, I estimated I had a mere three hours remaining of this gruelling ordeal, but I could feel the storm getting worse. Numerous participants had already thrown in the towel miles earlier.

Studying my map, I noticed the reservoir situated below, indicating I was nearing the end of my journey. However, a complication arose: reaching the final checkpoint required descending what appeared to be a steep incline. Yet, what seemed manageable on the map could be very different in reality, potentially leading to a fatal fall. Despite believing we had reached the lowest point of the cliff, I recognised the need to descend further to reach the path below. Hindered by darkness and a blinding snowstorm, I couldn't discern the terrain beneath me. Knowing failure to navigate this section would force me one hour back to find a new route, pushing me beyond the 20-hour cutoff point for selection.

Seated alongside my companions atop the cliff, silence enveloped us. Cold and exhaustion gnawed at our senses, with hypothermia creeping in and clouding our judgement. Despite this, my companions insisted on scouting for an alternative route. The storm had already consumed precious time, rendering further delays fatal. As the other two turned to start heading back into the storm, I peered over the edge, looking at the drop below me. I couldn't see its bottom as it was shrouded in darkness. Without thinking, I positioned my Bergen before me and surrendered to gravity's pull. I slid down the steep incline, gaining speed on the steep angle. Then, before I knew what was happening, I was in free fall, toppling over, no longer in control. "I am falling off a cliff!" I thought to myself. Almost before I could finish my thought and the scream had not even left my mouth, I face-planted heavily into the snow at the bottom. The snowdrift I was pulling my head out of had acted like a massive cushion for me.

I quickly checked myself and realised I was fine. I couldn't see the top of where I'd fallen from; everything was a whiteout. I shouted to the boys above me, letting them know I was okay. Within 30 seconds, they gathered their courage, and I heard two thuds, five seconds apart, as they landed heavily next to me. We exchanged nods of acknowledgement, shouldered our sodden bags on our frozen backs, and finished the final leg.

As we limped into the final checkpoint, we dropped our packs by a tree and rested for the first time in a long time. Pass or fail, I thought to myself, 'this is over.' My left arm was numb from the Bergen strap cutting into it, damaging nerves around my shoulder and neck. I held my rifle in my right hand, determined not to show any discomfort. Then, the Head of the Directing Staff came over to the three of us, sitting in a pile of dirty snow. He looked at us and then he extended his hand to me with a smile, and said, "Well done. You passed Selection." In what had been the goal for the last one and a half years and by far the nicest thing that the directing staff had ever said in all the months of shouting at us, I did not really react other than to smile back and say, "Thanks, Staff."

I stood as the sole survivor from our squadron of 30 to make it through the gruelling test week, alongside just two others from the entire country, originally comprising 102 recruits. With only two selection courses annually, it highlights the rarity of those who successfully navigate the SAS selection test week.

In fact, the experience of being told you have just successfully passed winter SAS physical selection is in no way dissimilar to reaching the summit of a mountain. You are just so happy that the pain has come to an end and that you are able just to stop what seems like a never-ending onslaught, that being told you passed or have made it to the summit does not really matter. It's moments like this or reaching the top of Everest that everyone assumes is an exhilarating moment when, in actual fact, the only thing that's running through your head at the time is "never again".

Only after, when you have had a beer in the warm comfort of a local pub and all danger and pain have long since passed, do you really feel a sense of satisfaction.

I never went on to complete the continuation phase with 21 SAS, perhaps having achieved what I wanted from the process and that now the big mountains were calling to me; however, passing physical SAS selection in the Hills that cold winter had really pushed me and taken my endurance further than I thought possible.

Now, high up in the Death Zone of Everest, cold, dehydrated, exhausted and at the end of my reserves, I remind myself that I have been in this position before. Although a very different beast, the special forces selection showed me that I could carry on moving even when I thought I was finished physically. It was like I had a blue print of how to react in the situation I am now in. I just have to keep on moving.

CHAPTER 14

Ghosts Frozen in Time

Still high up in the Death Zone, I was at the end of my reserves, fully aware that the "Death Zone" earns its name based on pure, hard facts. In this zone, life ceases to support itself, and your body begins to die. You have to play the roulette of getting out in time before your number comes up.

As if to remind me of this harsh reality, my head torch suddenly illuminated something unusual. The white, frozen landscape was interrupted by the faded clothes of a climber from the past, their half-submerged torso still fixed in position on the climbing route itself.

Having passed a few bodies, I began to look more closely at them, realising they each told their own sad story. Laying there, trapped and forever frozen in time, they hinted at the decade or century they came from. Some wore retro 1980s ski gear in bold, luminous colours, while others had the latest high-end mountaineering gear. Those with faded clothing in muted tones eluding back to the mid-20th century, the golden age of mountaineering. Their final moments seemed almost captured in an old-fashioned photograph from all those years ago.

The positions of the bodies, however, gave the greatest insight into their last moments. Some faced up the mountain as if still trying to climb, depicting their last desperate attempts to keep moving upward. One had made a makeshift shelter with sleeping bags and rucksacks, indicating a final but futile effort to survive. Sometimes, scattered climbing gear below the route suggested that some climbers had fallen thousands of feet off the North Face, never to be seen again. The most impactful for me was one who had curled into a foetal position, a last instinct for protection and warmth before death claimed them.

These bodies each tell a story of a possible end for me, chilling me with the thought that they could be a snapshot of my future. Would I be the lost climber in a crevasse, never to be found, or the one curled up in a ball after a slow death? These haunting images only strengthen my resolve. I need to keep my focus and concentrate on each and every step, just keep my focus.

Although these visceral images of dead climbers affect me, I strangely feel emotionally detached from them. It might seem cold, but the truth is that after many years in the police force, I've become desensitised to death. Their presence on the mountain no longer shocks me as it might have when I was younger. My years as a police officer involved dealing with countless deaths, making this grim reality almost routine.

Now, High up in this elevated graveyard, these grim past experiences of dealing with the dead as a Rookie cop now seem to serve me well whilst confronting these disturbing images.

After spending ten years in the police, dealing with sudden deaths and bodies in various states of decay, you become somewhat accustomed to it. Not in a pleasant way, as each case has its own horrors to confront, but over time and with more experience, you tend not to dwell on the gruesome memories. The shock value diminishes as your mind seeks to normalise this recurring event. However, some images are impossible to erase, and sometimes, without warning, they resurface as you close your eyes at night, haunting your thoughts.

I vividly recall my first incident involving a missing person case. Once it was determined that there was a serious concern for the man in question, I located his address and forced entry. Using what is known as the big red key, a battering ram, I quickly split the door from its hinges. As I entered, I was immediately met with an unfamiliar smell that would soon become all too recognisable throughout my police career.

The rotten flesh and internal decay of a human corpse emit a unique odour that is unmistakable when you breath it in, almost like a sweet, sickly, sticky smell that fills your nostrils and can take days to get rid of.

After gagging from the initial stench upon entering the door, I couldn't immediately pinpoint the source. Despite being a rookie, having recently joined the force, I knew without a doubt that this was the smell of a rotting corpse. Unable to find the missing man after searching the house, I decided to follow the smell, which led me back to one of the bedrooms I had already searched. The acrid, sweet smell drew me closer to the double bed in the centre of the room. Kneeling down beside it, my head nearly touching the dirty beige carpet, I lifted the overhanging bedsheet to peer underneath. There, just six inches from my face were the glassy, blue eyes of a decaying, rotten man. I didn't jump or scream; I simply lay there in shock for a few seconds. It was an odd moment, with both our heads lying side by side, almost as if we were about to engage in some pillow talk.

When discovering a body, particularly hidden under a bed, it is crucial to check for suspicious circumstances. This involves thoroughly examining the body, including turning it over, to identify any immediately obvious signs, such as a knife protruding from the back.

With the body being where it was, under the bed, I decided that I had to pull him out in order to have a look. I took hold of his arm and pulled. With a strong grip on his bare lower arm, I started walking backwards. Thinking I was being successful in pulling him out, I suddenly realise that all I have accomplished in doing is pulling his rotting arm flesh from his bones. I ended up with a putrid slop of skin and yellow-like blood and pus in my hands. This image, along with the smell, has never left me. When I'm alone, and my mind wonders on a sleepless night for no reason and without warning, the scene unfolds again in vivid technicolour, smell and touch.

Naturally, given the right conditions, a dead body left in a warm room for a few weeks will begin to decay. Eventually, all the fluids, flesh, and organs will break down into a sludge that soaks into the carpet.

When a body reaches this advanced state of decomposition, it becomes the responsibility of the Underwater Police dive team to handle it. Despite no water being involved, the decomposed state requires officers in full protective dive gear with oxygen masks to manage the hazardous mess and fumes. Often, they are left with the grim task of shovelling up most of the fluid and flesh, as it no longer has a body form.

I once considered joining the police underwater dive team, imagining it would be exciting. However, I quickly realised that most of the work involved recovering bodies, often in murky, sewage-filled rivers and canals where visibility is nonexistent. The only way to find a decaying corpse in such conditions is by touch.

As for the guy under the bed, he was in his 40s and had neglected his health. He contracted a blood infection and, with no friends or family to care for him, deteriorated gradually. He likely rolled off the bed and crawled beneath it, where he succumbed to a slow, lonely death, eventually curling into the foetal position as I found him.

Over the years, I've observed that the manner in which one dies often determines the final expression on one's face. On Everest, I've seen bodies curled up with their eyes closed, appearing to have drifted into a deep, almost contented sleep. However, this is not always the case. Some exits from this world are far less peaceful.

Two years into my service as a police officer, I responded to a routine report of a missing 40-year-old man. It was the end of a long night shift, and I arrived at his address alone just as dawn was breaking over a rural area west of Bristol. A cold mist enveloped the property, giving it a spooky, isolated feel. I knocked on the door, but there was no answer. Circling the house, I searched for a way to gain entry.

With two years on the job, I had honed my skills in identifying weak points on properties for entry. A short climb to a first-floor window, often left slightly open, usually yielded success. At the back of this property, I spotted some wooden-framed windows that seemed vulnerable. Using my police-issue baton (asp), I pried the window open and crawled through the narrow opening on my belly. Inside, it was nearly pitch black, with only a few faint rays of early morning light filtering in. Without a torch, I moved slowly, my hand outstretched to avoid collisions, while my eyes struggled to adapt to the darkness. Suddenly, my right hand struck a solid object covered in plastic. I prodded it, feeling something spongy. I froze, squinting hard into the darkness. As my eyes adjusted, the horrific scene before me revealed itself.

The scene before me could best be described as a face resembling the "scream painting" just staring back at me, only a foot away. Jumping in shock, I fell backwards in an instinctive bid to try to get away, letting out a sharp, fearful yelp in the process. I held my breath whilst lying on the carpet floor, almost waiting for something to happen. After ten seconds, I got to my feet and hesitantly approached. In front of me stood a man with a clear plastic bag over his head, sealed with tape around his neck. His mouth was wide open as if frozen in a scream, with the plastic tightly sucked into his mouth. His eyes were wide open, bulging out of their sockets. It resembled a scene from a horror movie. The spongy objects I had prodded earlier must have been his eyes. I moved to the wall and felt my way around the room, tracing the textured wallpaper until I found the light switch. With the room now illuminated, everything became clear. A small 5 ft hose pipe, taped securely inside the bag, led to a large canister marked "Helium" in bold letters. Judging by his skin colour and the rigidity of his body, I estimated he had been dead for about 24 hours. Despite this, I couldn't shake the feeling that he might suddenly spring to life.

As I tentatively sat down on the sofa next to him, half expecting him to answer, I said out loud, "Why did you do that?" I think in an effort to calm my nerves.

As I glanced around his beige, modern lounge, furnished with Ikea pieces, my eyes caught photos of his children on the walls. In those pictures, he appeared as a younger man, clearly in better times, standing on a windswept beach with a broad smile, a stark contrast to the tormented figure sitting next to me.

On the coffee table in front of me, his death note was openly displayed. Reading the letter, I saw it was a tale of pain and farewells to his children, stating he could not take it anymore, yet never hinting at the reasons why. I couldn't help but question what events could lead someone to end it all like that.

What often goes unspoken in the police is the long wait that follows the discovery of a dead body. Until the CSI team and medical professionals arrive to certify the death, an officer can spend hours alone with the dead.

Again, still overwhelmed by the situation and in disbelief, I speak to him, asking, "Why did you do it?"

It's not uncommon to have a conversation with the dead in such circumstances. I've spoken to many police officers who have done this. Situations like these aren't covered in any training manual; you simply do what feels right to help you cope with the tragedy laid out before you.

In this profession, I have witnessed hundreds of deaths in

various forms. It is only natural, then, to ponder the worst ways to die, almost creating a morbid list of the most dreadful ends. From those who have set themselves on fire, fallen victim to knife attacks, or met with fatal accidents on icy roads on their way to work one morning, the shock and pain of their final moments are often imprinted on their faces like death masks. In contrast, the frozen faces of the dead on Everest curled up and appearing to sleep, seem much calmer. Their closed eyes and relaxed expressions suggest a peaceful end. I believe this is due to their final moments being less about sudden, intense pain and more about the slow onset of altitude sickness. This brings a sense of delirium, a detachment from reality, combined with hypothermia, leading them to drift into a dream-filled deep sleep.

As they lay there on the mountain with their eyes closed, holding a relaxed expression, it brings me some comfort of sorts, knowing they were not really aware of their imminent end.

Deep down, I wonder if I'm just trying to comfort myself with these stories.

I'm making good progress, and with my pace slightly faster, I have moved ahead of Alex. The temperature has dropped further to at least minus 35 degrees, but for the first time in a long time, I feel it's all going to plan. I start to mutter to myself, "I'm going to do this; I'm going to get to the top of this mountain."

As I ascend over the crest of the gully, I firmly drive my ice axe into the snow. Surprisingly, the sharp steel point doesn't penetrate as deeply as anticipated, offering an unusual sensation. Nevertheless, it just about secures me. Or so I assume. Horror grips me as I realise my anchor is a frozen corpse. The deceased climber's body lies mostly submerged, with only the upper part of the head and torso visible mere centimetres away. The thin air of high altitude already slows my thoughts. With my ice axe lodged in the frozen flesh, I pause, removing my oxygen mask to gasp the frigid air. After a moment and my initial shock calms, I muster my resolve, delicately extracting my axe from the body with cautious wiggles. I slowly start to move up, happy to forget the last horror-filled minute, when, in the dark distance about 50 metres ahead of me, I see a glimmer of red light. Curious, I approach, my thoughts racing. Suddenly, a strange, screaming noise echoes around the mountain, etching itself into my memory forever.

CHAPTER 15

Shadow Man

At 8,700 metres, the mountain air hangs eerily still, the night sky awash with a multitude of stars. It's 4:30 a.m. The only sound breaking the silence is the rhythmic crunch of my crampons against the icy snow, a steady backbeat in the darkness for the last hour. Suddenly, the piercing scream-like noise slices through the frozen air once again, breaking the deafening silence.

I suddenly regret climbing alone. I ask myself why I've pushed on again and left Alex behind.

I try to recover myself by breathing deeply and trying to process the noise. A split second later, I freeze to the spot as the shill scream echoes across the mountain once more. I don't like being on my own.

I don't know who or even what it is or where it's coming from, but as I climb up, the screaming gets louder. I approach cautiously and slow my pace, scanning my weak head torch beam of light around me to see what's making this sound. My mind is awash with confusion and fear, "What's making that noise?" "Is it human?" "It has to be." I think to myself in a bid to reduce the increasing tension building in me. As I climb over a snow-dusted rock, a red glow catches my eye once more, giving the snow around a sinister feeling. Within this eerie red glow, something emerges, nestled on a narrow ledge of snow, barely ten metres ahead of me.

As I approach, almost tip-toeing on my crampons in anticipation, my head torch takes over the red glow and lights up what appears to be a big pile of red fabric lying in the white snow. "What is that?" I mutter to myself, "Perhaps a collapsed tent." Suddenly, as I fixate on the crimson object, it emits a piercing shriek and shifts position. I'm paralysed, my breath caught in my throat, as I gaze in disbelief, trying to comprehend the unfolding scene. Slowly, the truth dawns on me; I'm starring at a man in a red down jacket, sprawled on the snow. His curled-up form resembles a big red ball, accentuated by the glow of his head torch set to red light mode. With cautious steps, I inch closer, half-expecting him to jump up. Yet, with another sudden wail, more shrilled this time, I halt, rooted to the spot. It feels like I just stared at him for 2 minutes, but in reality, it was probably more like 30 seconds. My mind clouded, feeling the oppressive weight of altitude sickness creeping in once more.

The man's utterances are disjointed, consisting of groans and random screams that are both unsettling and chilling. I kneel beside him, lifting the hood of his down jacket to reveal his face. His oxygen mask hangs loosely under his chin, and he lacks goggles. Upon closer inspection, I notice his wide, vacant stare directed towards me, yet it feels as if he's looking through me like he does not know I'm there. As I focus on his distant gaze, he emits a piercing shriek devoid of discernible words. This time, the shriek is deafening.

As the shriek stops, complete silence envelopes us again. With my fear calming down, I look closer and realise that I recognise who it is. I was staring at Jack, my friend from basecamp.

Looking at Jack, I realise he's oblivious to my presence, unresponsive to my attempts to gain his attention. Calling his name yields no reaction; his gaze remains fixed, distant, as if peering through me. Despite my efforts to secure his oxygen mask, he persistently removes it.

Anchored by my crampons in the snow, I feel helpless, unsure of what else to do but remain by his side on the narrow ledge. I tread cautiously, mindful not to disturb the precarious balance on the one-metre-wide platform, with a sheer 3,000-foot drop below us of the North face.

Whilst perched here in my precarious spot, staring out into the darkness, I feel detached from the scene before me, almost questioning if it's real.

Slowly, in my altitude-fogged mind, much like putting pieces of a puzzle together, the realisation of the significance of the events transpiring becomes inescapable. Jack is dying.

Jack is in the later throes of High-Altitude Cerebral Oedema.

I've encountered the initial symptoms of HACE firsthand and observed them in numerous others, where an excess of blood rushes to the brain in an attempt to maintain oxygen levels. Regrettably, this process exacerbates the situation by exerting greater pressure on the brain. Consequently, it precipitates a swift decline in both physical and cognitive function, often culminating in coma and, ultimately, death.

I sit there feeling pretty hopeless.

As I stand here in my exposed spot with a man fighting for his life to my right and the 3,000 ft abyss just centimetres to my left, the stark reality of my situation hits me. Is this the end of my summit bid? Am I now part of what looks like a doomed rescue attempt?

A wave of disappointment crashes over me instantly. Three years of my life have led to this single point. Nausea churns in my stomach as the weight of this realisation sinks in. Losing even an hour here could spell the end of my summit bid. As I stand high on the mountain, consumed by my selfish desire for the summit, I nearly forget about the dying man lying at my feet.

I rapidly assess my options, trying to formulate a plan. Alone in the darkness high up in Everest's Death Zone, I'm with an injured man who can't climb or walk. The situation is dire. I can barely move my own body in this oxygen-starved environment, let alone carry another. I consider the possibility of dragging Jack down.

I then shine my torch down the mountain and see the sheer drop below me, realising that our situation is hopeless. Jack cannot speak or walk; if I try to move him, he will slide straight off and likely drag me with him despite the rope. Every scenario I imagine, even strapping him tightly to my body, leads to the same grim conclusion: it won't work. We are too high up on steep ground, and the most probable outcome is both of us dying in the attempt. Even if I could drag him, it would take hours to descend just a hundred metres, and by then, I would be succumbing to serious altitude sickness. The Death Zone spares no one; anyone who stays here too long dies.

Still perched on the ledge beside Jack, with no more ideas on how to get him to safety, I resigned myself to stay with him. It wasn't a conscious decision but rather a result of not knowing what else to do.

As my tired mind starts to drift, I suddenly hear some shuffling up above me. A Sherpa then pops his head over a ledge 20 metres above me and says, "Hello, sir," in a very polite, calm way, not befitting the intense circumstances. I climb up to him where he explains that he was with Jack earlier when he was unwell. The Sherpa then starts saying, "It's no good, finished," in broken English, referring to jack and his imminent demise.

The Sherpa, with his light blue down jacket, continues saying, "It's OK, I give him hot chocolate." I'm left dumfounded and confused as to how hot chocolate is going to resolve this predicament in any way. The Sherpa just shakes his head and says, "Not good." I stand there for a minute, trying to process the new information I have just been presented with. It then dawns on me that now there are two of us it might be possible to try and move Jack. I ask the Sherpa if this is an option, but he replies very firmly, "No possible, no walk." He then remarks again that he has given Jack hot chocolate and nods in approval. I shoot the Sherpa a bemused look at his persistent comments about hot chocolate, but he was right, and I knew it. In Jack's current state, drifting in and out of consciousness, it was clear that two or even three people would not be able to get him down. Any attempt would likely result in injury or death for those who tried. Offering hot chocolate was a gesture of comfort for Jack's remaining time and a sign that the Sherpa had accepted Jack's fate. I ask if he has any Dex, a steroid injection of Dexamethasone, which is known to help with cerebral altitude sickness. The Sherpa just replied, "Yes, already given, no good."

As the Sherpa makes this comment, I let out a deep sigh, resigning myself to the fact that there is nothing more I can do. The only thought that runs through my mind is that my summit attempt is finished, and all I can do now is sit here and wait for him to die.

Unlike the hero narrative that a Hollywood blockbuster would have you believe, where you try at all costs to save the dying climber, the stark reality is I am left feeling denied of choice and rather impotent.

For another 45 minutes, I stayed in my precarious position on the mountain's side, with the tips of my crampons digging into the snow. My ice axe was deeply embedded, its sharp point biting into the ice. Using the hand strap of the axe, I secured myself as best as possible, tying it to my harness.

During this time on his small ledge, Jack has stayed silent while the Sherpa has climbed to a position above, out of sight. Time crawls by in the stillness, broken only by the sound of my shivering in the minus-35-degree air.

Feeling very alone, I realise that inaction means death for me as well. I've already concluded that rescuing Jack, given his condition and location, is impossible. This leaves me with two options: wait with him until he dies, then descend alone, or continue to the summit. Weakness is setting in; the time spent here has caused me to get cold and worsened the effects of the altitude on my body.

Can I carry on my summit bid? If I continue up, I still have

3 hours of climbing to get to the top and then another 10 hours of descent.

How will I be judged if I carry on and leave a dying man? This fear of condemnation by the Armchair Everest community is ever-present. I remember the outrage following the 1996 disaster when climbers were accused of walking past the dying to reach the summit. Practical arguments seem to be disregarded, and climbers hesitate to voice their true thoughts during such dire moments.

I feel my mind growing weary as the hypoxia from the thin air begins to starve my brain, and cerebral oedema starts to take hold. I've been here too long. Suddenly, out of the corner of my right eye, I see a shadowy figure standing tall about five metres ahead. When I direct my head torch at the figure, it almost becomes harder to see and disappears. As I move the beam of light, the dark shadow reveals itself as a human-like form. I can make out a head and arms but without any detail. The dark figure stands tall, taller than a man, but I have no sense of perspective; I don't know how far away it is. Suddenly, the figure moves one of its arms in a beckoning motion, inviting me to come closer up the mountain. I blink repeatedly, unable to believe what I'm seeing. When I look again with my head torch, the shadowy figure is gone. This must be my oxygen-starved mind playing tricks, but deep down, I know I've seen him. I shake my head, trying to regain my senses as new focus returns to me.

"I still want this," I think to myself; there is nothing more I can do here. A chilling realisation grips me as the relentless obsession resurfaces. It hits me hard that this desolate landscape, situated eight and a half kilometres above ground, renders us utterly isolated. In this remote corner of the world, it's just us, with no witnesses to our actions. If I were to simply bypass him and forge ahead, no one would ever know. In my calculating mind, I understand that even the Sherpa has accepted the grim reality, resigning himself to the inevitability of our situation. With this understanding, my dark desire to press onward would remain a secret, dying on this snow-covered slope along with Jack.

As I form a plan with these unsettling thoughts, pushing aside the mysterious shadow man beckoning me forward, a surge of determination courses through me. The Summit calls to me once more, reigniting my drive. Despite the darkness lingering at the edges of my mind, I find myself compelled by the challenge ahead. The fever of the Summit grips me anew, fuelling my resolve. I can still do this.

The term "Summit fever" is often banded around as a buzz word, but it is very real. It's an unrelenting ache that drives you forward, a desire to override all pain and rational thought. It allows you to put one foot in front of the other, moving up, always up with one single purpose of reaching the top. This fever is the reason for many successful summits, but its single mindedness is also the result of many of the disasters in mountaineering.

Lost in the allure of summit conquest yet again, my thoughts are saturated with the imagined glory of reaching the top. Abruptly, Jack lets out a heavy groan, which seems like a stark reminder of his presence beside me. Instantly, a wave of guilt washes over me, harshly jolting me back to the grim reality of the situation.

Once more, I find myself grappling with internal conflict. While I've logically concluded that there's no feasible way to rescue him, I can't shake the unsettling truth that my choice to press forward conveniently aligns with my selfish ambition to reach the summit.

In grappling with the decision looming before me, I attempt to justify our predicament. Jack and I had both signed up to the understanding that you may not come home. Yet, deep down, I acknowledge that my efforts to justify our choices serve more as a shield against criticism from others later on. Despite this internal struggle, I find resolve in the certainty of my decision. Scanning the surroundings, I half-expect to encounter my shadow man once more, perhaps seeking reassurance or absolution. But I can't see him anymore. Nevertheless, my course is set. I've resolved to leave Jack behind and press on towards the summit.

It takes me about 5 minutes to climb up to the Sherpa, and without thinking, I ask again, "Can I help?" Although I'm anticipating that he will probably reply with a hot chocolate comment I'm suddenly dreading his response. What if he changes his mind and says yes? Then I'm committed. I curse myself inside, thinking, "Why did I ask again?" In a split second, I envisage a bumbled attempt to try and move Jack only to get him 100 metres or so in a failed rescue and then return home to say I didn't make it. I try to explain the reason why, with no-one really being interested, as they stopped listening to my excuse at the point when I said I did not make it to the top.

The Sherpa turns to me and again says, "No good." He then starts talking about hot chocolate, but I switch off. My mind is now focused elsewhere. Is this my green light to continue? Even if it means leaving a dying man.

Hurriedly, I descend to Jack on the ledge, swiftly preparing myself by donning my rucksack once more. A sense of urgency consumes me as I realise the precious time that has slipped away. Impatience gnaws at me as I become acutely aware of my dwindling oxygen supply and the valuable time I have lost.

Out of nowhere, Alex then suddenly appears 10 metres below me, seemingly unaware of the grave situation, but his silence indicates he knows it's bad.

In the calm silence, I lower my oxygen mask beneath my chin and push back the hood of my thick jacket, revealing my head to the biting cold. Immediately, the freezing air stings my exposed face. With my bulky, mittened glove, I gently lift Jack's head, ensuring a clear view of his face. His expression is frozen, and his head is stiff. Our faces are mere inches apart, our eyes locked in an unyielding gaze. Yet, despite our proximity, his haunting stare seems to penetrate right through me. I can't see or hear any breath come from his mouth. I say quietly, "I'm gonna move on." He does not acknowledge me. I say again, "I'm moving on now," almost wanting his approval or acknowledgement, but I cannot pretend there is any. As I attempt to move my right foot, I realise it's entangled in something. Glancing downwards, I notice Jack's gloved hand gripping my boot tightly. It's evident he's reluctant to let me proceed; deep within his subconscious, he clings to life desperately.

In a moment of inner conflict, I find myself murmuring, almost pleading for assistance to extricate myself from this predicament. Uncertain of my audience, I strike a silent bargain with myself and anyone listening: if granted safe passage to the summit, I vow eternal gratitude and readiness to pay any price. It's as if I need permission to move on. I look around for the shadow man; I repeatedly mutter under my breath, "Just get me to the top," then all of a sudden, almost without reasoning, I feel a wave of acceptance and determination as if permission to move has been granted. It feels like I just struck the darkest of all deals. Gazing down at Jack's weakening hold on my boot, I retract my foot almost effortlessly, witnessing his lifeless hand slip onto the snow.

I plunge my ice axe into the steep ice high above me and, in doing so, step over Jack's almost lifeless body. Alex follows me in silence.

After much contemplation and wavering, the initial action of stepping past Jack marked a turning point, easing subsequent steps until the path ahead became resolute. With each metre conquered, determination surged within me, reaffirming my course. As I ascended, the impending reality of Jack's fate loomed, strangely justifying my decision to press onward. Grateful for the unseen force that propelled me forward, I began to distance myself from the weight of the desperate bargain struck for summit success. The details of the desperate deal are already fading as I forge ahead, leaving it behind in pursuit of the summit.

As I find my rhythm once more and optimism begins to resurface, a familiar noise pierces the air, causing me to halt in my tracks. The shrill shriek, now ingrained in my memory, sends shivers down my spine. Amidst the chaos, I can just make out a single word. The sound reverberates across the mountain, then falls deathly quiet. I stand motionless, holding my breath, waiting to hear if there will be anymore sound. Yet, there's only silence, enveloping me in feelings of confusion and self-doubt. Jack is still very much alive.

Jack grapples with the final delusions of cerebral altitude sickness. Drifting in and out of consciousness, he clings fiercely to one singular obsession. In his last fleeting moments of lucidity on that cold, dark night was the word "Summit". The echo of that haunting utterance lingers in my memory, a testament to the truly powerful drive to reach the top. It's a stark reminder that even in the face of impending death, the allure of the summit remains unbroken.

I turn to face the mountain and start to move up. The hard ground becomes near vertical as I plunge my ice axe into the snow, desperately trying to lose myself in the physical effort of climbing.

Alex and I are back together, and I'm moving away from the tragedy. I'm almost relieved to forget what just happened, knowing that no one will ever know about the secret deal I made up here in the Death Zone to keep my summit dream alive at all costs. I want to erase this tragedy and the encounter with the strange shadow man from my memory, pretending it never happened.

CHAPTER 16

Frozen Eye Balls

It's been over an hour since I left Jack. At 8,750 metres, my climb up the North East Ridge of Everest shifts direction. Now, it leads me to a narrow ledge, just centimetres wide and stretching 100 metres along Everest's North Face. I must traverse this ledge to reach the route that ascends to the final section towards the summit.

However, the ledge is terrifyingly exposed. As I edge sideways, the 2 cm front steel points of my crampons bite into the ice, with a 3,000 ft drop below me. The path along the ledge means I have to unclip from the rope at intervals, leaving me without protection as I navigate it.

Every now and then, I look down, feeling a bit sick for doing so. Although I can't see all the way to the bottom, I know for sure that a fall means certain death as I imagine tumbling into the dark silence below me.

As the wind intensifies, I feel the cold biting through me. Despite my thick balaclava and merino wool hat, nothing stops the chill from seeping in. My vision begins to blur, and the path ahead becomes obscured. Anxiety sets in as I recognise this sight loss is an early symptom of High-Altitude Cerebral Oedema. Lifting my goggles, I rub my eyes, only to realise that condensation has built up inside. I'm slightly relieved that it's my goggles and not my eyes, but each time I wipe the condensation away, it reappears within minutes.

The wind starts to blow ever stronger, and with it, the temperature plummets. To my frustration, the condensation freezes on the inside of my goggles, leaving them completely frosted. I can't see through them at all. I continue, blind, feeling my way along the North Face wall with my gloves while my ice axe dangles from the strap like a blind man's cane. It's becoming ridiculous; twice within the next minute, I put my right foot over the edge, nearly falling. I have to remove the goggles. Reluctantly, I expose my eyes to the elements and carry on climbing. My head torch illuminates the thin traverse ahead. Despite the cold, I feel encouraged by the immediate advantage of restored vision on such a tricky section.

I know removing my goggles in this freezing air temperature of minus 40 degrees Celsius is a dangerous move, especially in the coldest part of the night. Despite the risk, I have no choice. I need to see the precarious route ahead of me.

After about 5 minutes without my goggles, I'm making good progress along the traverse, happy with my decision.

All of a sudden, I realise that I cannot blink, and my vision is starting to go blurry. I franticly try to close my eyes, straining to force this seemingly straightforward eyelid action.

I mutter to myself in a state of alarm and realisation, "My eyes have frozen!" "I'm going blind." I shout louder, "My eyes are frozen!" I sit down perched precariously on the edge with my back to the rock and feet dangling off the 3,000 ft drop. The height of the drop beneath me is of little consequence now as I can't see the danger. I'm blind.

I bury my head in my thick green down jacket, forcing my frozen eyelids shut and covering them with my big mitten gloves in an attempt to warm them up. Panic sets in as I struggle to breathe; my mask isn't providing any oxygen. I remove my right glove and feel the ice build-up on the oxygen regulator hose leading to my mask. My oxygen system is frozen. The only sound around me is the wind, which is picking up speed and whipping fiercely.

I tell myself to rise. I then start a process of blindly fumbling and inching my way along the North Face of Everest, each step a struggle. Every other movement brings me to my knees. Blind from frozen eyes and deprived of oxygen, I'm reduced to crawling, yet I persist, inching closer to my goal. I keep convincing myself that success is still within reach. However, with every fumbled step, the harsh reality sets in: I am alone, blind, and without oxygen in one of the most unforgiving places on Earth. The truth becomes clear: I am as good as dead.

The situation feels desperate, but I'm consumed with one overriding thought: just keep moving up.

Permanently losing your sight at high altitude is, undeniably, a death sentence. Surprisingly, vision loss is a common occurrence in the Death Zone, marking the beginning of a downward spiral that almost invariably results in a fatal outcome.

With my eyes frozen and my vision black, I strain to peer along the narrow ledge. Suddenly, a glimmer of brightness catches my eye on the right. At first, I can't quite fathom what I'm seeing.

Just as despair begins to settle in, I realise it's the sun rising in the East. The first rays of dawn strike my face, hard to describe, but feels like a blanket of warmth, both physical and emotional, enveloping me. After about five minutes of staring at the new sun, I begin to feel my eye balls defrosting, an odd sensation that leaves them bruised and gritty, as if still filled with ice granules.

Another 15 minutes pass and the limited oxygen flow from my regulator kicks in, thawed by the sun's rays. Compared to 20 minutes ago, I can now see and breathe. With my vision clear and oxygen flowing, I push onward, invigorated by the newfound warmth and strength of the rising sun.

From all the expeditions I've undertaken over the years, I've developed a profound appreciation for the transformative power of a sunrise. Only in those moments when you're at your lowest, coldest, and farthest from home, nearing the end of your strength, do you truly grasp the life-giving power the sun has.

A wave of optimism washes over me as my eyes adjust to the light of a new day. I spot someone lying down, resting just ten feet ahead, and feel a surge of relief; it's the first person I've seen in quite a while, having been separated from Alex for the past hour. As I draw nearer, the stark reality hits me: I'm looking at a dead body. Partially submerged in snow, the figure wears a faded blue jacket. His face darkened and dehydrated by the relentless sun, with exposed teeth down to his receding gums, resembles something out of a horror film.

I have to say this was not the greatest sight to have on regaining my vision, but it does stop me from drifting and gives me more resolve to focus and to keep pushing harder.

As I reach the end of the traverse, the route then takes a direct line up the North Face. I'm getting close now; it's been nearly ten hours since I left camp, and I've not eaten or drunk anything. The small amount of water I have is frozen solid.

Before departing the last camp, we set ourselves a ten-hour limit to reach the summit. This was the cut-off time, based on our oxygen and physical reserves. Breaking these timing rules means risking not making it back down. Despite knowing the risks, I have secretly decided to push past the time limit. The deal I made with someone or something in the dead of night only a few hours ago to allow me to continue is driving me to disregard the rules. My sole focus is to reach the summit of Everest and worry about the rest later. All the carefully laid plans and promises I made to turn back if the time limit was reached have been abandoned. Like so many before me, breaking my own rules about turn-around time can come at a great cost.

I'm aware of how my mindset is so different now from when I started this trip all those months ago; gone are the fears, now I'm prepared to risk it all.

I climb on to the balcony section of the North Face, which is a small, relatively flat area covered in snow close to the summit. Seb, my American doctor team mate, is on his descent. He is all smiles. I try to put on a cheery face; he takes a snap and says, pointing, "It's just up there."

I look up and say, "I'm going up; let's get this done; see you in a while." I give him the thumbs up in some attempt of false bravado that everything is alright, but I'm still shaken from losing my sight only 45 minutes ago. Even though I've been with these guys for almost three months, I still don't want to show weakness or lose face.

As I edge past Seb to conquer the final 50 metres to the summit, my right crampon unexpectedly falls off. What should be a simple two-minute fix turns into a gruelling 10-minute ordeal. The seemingly easy task of securing the crampon and tightening a few straps drains my energy completely. Then, the reason for my struggle becomes clear: checking my oxygen regulator, I see it's on zero, completely empty. That's it, I think to myself. With nothing more I can do, I try to push it out of my mind, focusing on the summit.

With a mere 40 metres remaining, now almost touching distance to the summit, it still takes me about 15 minutes. The snow is deep in places, and the slope steepens as I inch closer, pausing with every step, gasping the thin air, trying to grasp whatever oxygen remains at this altitude.

I see the summit; there are red and blue prayer flags littered around a small snow cap area no bigger than a snooker table. Only 10 metres to go; still, it seems to take a few minutes.

I take my final steps and plant my right foot on the summit. I'm standing at the highest point. I don't say or do anything; I'm simply numb, breathing deeply and feeling slightly light-headed. Alone, I stare blankly at the horizon, grateful that the pain in my lungs and body has ceased. I'm thankful for the rest but still need to breathe deeply, drawing in whatever thin air I can.

With all my past challenges and the hardships they had brought, it felt as if they had now all come together to allow me to reach the top of Everest.

It wasn't a moment of celebration and wonder but rather one of profound relief that I had finally arrived after a long and arduous journey. As I exhale a frosty breath of thin, jet stream air, I feel the weight of the years-long burden to reach this summit melt away.

I'm alone on the summit when I hear someone panting coming from below me over the other side of the summit. A big lad 6 ft tall with a ginger beard and shaggy hair just appears on the Summit from the Nepalese south side route. He takes a breath and then shouts, "Yeah," really, really loudly, as if he is going to explode. I smile to myself and think, "American." He had just spent the last two months in another country, Nepal, doing the same as me, battling his fear in the cold and finally reaching the climax of his journey to the summit.

In this big life-defining moment, we both turn to each other, only a foot apart, on the summit of the World and in turn just say "Alright," in a quiet, low manner, greeting like we just bumped into each other in the local park or something.

I'm not entirely sure what the etiquette really is, but we are both knackered and didn't have the energy for much else.

The truth is, when I look back on my summit moments from climbing mountains around the world, I don't have many memories of elation or marvelling at the view. Instead, you're so overwhelmed with relief that you can finally breathe without pain and rest for a while. It's no different from finishing a hard run or workout when your body is instantly flooded with endorphins, nature's own little opiates. It's a quiet, euphoric moment, feeling high in a high place. However, this feeling quickly fades, replaced by the daunting realisation that you're only halfway and utterly exhausted. You become acutely aware that most deaths occur on the descent.

Looking back, the image in my mind is of a beautiful sunrise on the summit of Everest, with Makalu to the east and the Tibetan plateau stretching out 100 miles to the north. But in truth, these are not the real images. The photos from the summit show the sunrise and the triumphant faces, and this image has almost replaced the reality of the underwhelming feeling I experienced. It's like those smiling holiday photos where memories are shaped by the pictures rather than the actual events.

Alex arrives about 10 minutes after me on the summit. We don't talk much apart from, "Well done mate." We take some pictures, and then Alex's batteries run out after about three shots; Alex starts to change them very slowly, as is the only way to do things up here.

Then, about six Chinese climbers appear over the ridge and take over the small summit spot. They're loud and oblivious to our presence. I start getting irate with Alex for taking so long and urge him to hurry up, which in turn agitates him. Suddenly, it's nothing like the serene Everest summit experience I had imagined.

After about 25 minutes on the summit, annoyed with everyone, I realise that every extra minute here is gambling with my life. Standing on the highest point on Earth without supplemental oxygen, I know it's time to get moving.

I know I have to stay switched on. I remind myself that I'm only halfway. By now, I'm severely dehydrated, and the altitude is slowing my thought process by affecting my logical brain function. I'm acutely aware of the grim statistics of mountain descents. Most accidents happen on the way down, driven by exhaustion and switching off mentally. I'm determined not to become just another death number. I just need to keep my focus.

Top: Tibetan locals showing what they think about western climbers.

Bottom: Base camp yoga sessions with Everest inbetween Max's legs.

Dom all clean on arrival at Base Camp Northside, Tibet.

Top: Yaks helping to carry the load through the long first section to interim camp and ABC.

Bottom: ABC (6,400 metres).

The Puja ceremony with the Sherpas to bless our equipment
and ourselves before departing for summit push.

Top left: Ice training on the glacier ice at ABC.

Top right: Dom testing oxygen equipment at ABC before the summit push.

Bottom: Dom and Alex disappearing into the ice on the North Col on the summit push (just below 7,000 metres).

Dom leading with other team members on the North Col.

Good weather window prompts a summit push, with many teams having the same idea. Midway between Camp 1 and Camp 2 (7,500 metres).

Top: Camp 2 (7,800 metres). View of Tibetan plateau rolling off to the North.

Bottom: Exhausted at camp 3 (8,300 metres). Jack in centre.

Dom at first light close to the summit (8,750 metres). Curvature of Earth visible on the horizon. Two hours after leaving Jack.

Top: First sight of the summit.

Bottom left: Dom standing on the summit of Everest (8,848 metres). 7:30 am (oxygen mask has frozen).

Bottom right: Descending from the 2nd step after summit, passing the body of a climber from a past expeditions.

Down safe from the North Col after successful summit, Coke in hand and feeling the weight lifted from my shoulders.

CHAPTER 17

In the Cold Light of Day

I push down the mountain, my confidence growing with each step. My pace quickens as I navigate the terrain, once again finding myself alone. Rounding a large rock buttress, I spot a climber ascending the steep ice gully towards me. They stand out vividly in their bright red-down gear. Baffled by the scene in front of me, a series of questions race through my mind: What the hell is he doing? Where's he come from? Maybe he is doing another route? Or am I on the wrong route?

As I draw nearer, the stark reality hits me: the climber isn't moving. Recognition strikes like a hammer blow; it's Jack. The memory of the earlier incident, obscured by the night and my own mental barriers, resurfaces with brutal clarity. Just hours ago, his piercing scream had echoed in the darkness as I left him behind. I had forced myself to suppress the horror of that moment, but now, faced with his motionless form, the grim truth is impossible to ignore.

In my tired oxygen-starved mind, the morning light shows me in full technicolour the night's events that I could happily have consigned to a nightmare were, in fact, deadly reality.

Jack's position is directly below the main route, about two metres down from where I'm standing. He's wedged in a small, near-vertical gully, attached by some ropes. The scene before me seems surreal; it almost looks like he's merely taking a break. Unlike the other bodies I've passed, Jack appears strikingly different. The vivid red of his down jacket stands out sharply against the snow, and his posture suggests he could spring into action at any moment, as if about to dig in his crampon or plant his ice axe.

I approach cautiously, half expecting him to move.

Of course, this was not the case, and Jack had passed away in the night shortly after I left him.

His position is now about six feet below where I had seen him five hours earlier. His team, out of respect, had moved him off the main route. They wanted to ensure that in the frozen years to come, climbers wouldn't have to step on or over him as they passed.

In truth, "moved" is a polite phrase, as essentially the Sherpa and some of his team, later that night after he had died, pushed him off the edge with ropes attached so he would not fall too far. As undignified as this may seem, it was a practical resting place that involved much physical effort from his team members.

The night's drama surges back into my consciousness, a wave of panicked guilt engulfing my thoughts. Only hours ago, in the enveloping darkness, I had pushed the memory aside, but now, in the stark light of day, the nightmare feels all too real. There's no escaping the reality that confronts me. The pact I made with myself to reach the summit at any cost now stands brutally clear and is inescapable.

My mind races, anticipating the explanations I'll need to provide for my actions that night. I tell myself, "Keep the story short." I plan to explain how I paused and realised that Jack was beyond help, with no chance of rescue, and how I still offered my assistance.

Despite my attempts to justify my actions, a nagging truth lingered in the back of my mind: I had felt a twisted sense of elation, almost happiness when I chose to press on towards the summit. It was as if something had granted me permission to continue my single-minded pursuit. Deep down, I knew there was likely nothing I could do to change the situation, but the harsh reality remained: I had left a dying man at my feet to chase the summit.

I had seized on the answer from the Sherpa to continue with my summit bid as a definitive response and grabbed with both hands the opportunity to pursue my quest regardless. The permission for me to continue seemingly coming from an unknown place. It felt as if something or someone could sense my weakness of desire to summit at any cost. The memory of me pleading in the night, making a deal to get me to the top, whatever the price, was coming back to me. Who had I been speaking to in my oxygen-starved mind? Who or what was the Shadow Man beckoning me up? With the harsh light of the mountain sun rays now reflecting their power off the brilliant white snow, it all seems very surreal, almost as if last night's tragedy had just been a confused nightmare.

Gazing at Jack, his final resting place amidst the unforgiving landscape, doubt gnaws at me. Was I too hasty in deferring to the Sherpa's judgement? Just because he deemed the situation hopeless didn't render me devoid of my own decision making. With years of mountaineering expertise behind me, I possessed the capacity for independent thought. Yet, in that critical moment, I relinquished my role as a decision-maker, opting instead to defer to another's assessment to suit my ends.

Perhaps I deferred to his judgement, though deep down, I knew, based on my own assessment, that attempting a rescue would likely be futile. Or perhaps, if I'm honest with myself, the decision not to assist was merely a convenient excuse, an easy justification to continue ascending the mountain after the Shadow Man's invitation to move up.

Thoughts swirl in my mind, contemplating whether his now cold body would ever depart this desolate place. The scattered array of lifeless bodies I had just passed served as a grim reminder. This, I knew, was Jack's final resting place. As I gaze out over the vast expanse stretching hundreds of miles across the Tibetan plateau, I attempt to find solace in the notion that there are worse places for one's eternal slumber.

The challenges inherent in high-altitude operations became starkly evident during Stephan's descent. Just two hours behind me, accompanied by Marcus, he was making his way down after a successful summit attempt. Stephan's original plan was to retrieve personal effects belonging to Paul, his climbing partner, who tragically lost his life on the mountain the year before, with the intention of returning them to Paul's family. Despite a year of planning and being mere feet away from Paul's resting place, Stephan found himself unable to fulfil this objective. The daunting task of navigating the treacherous terrain just metres off the established route and extracting items from his backpack proved to be an insurmountable challenge at such extreme altitudes.

As I sit here, my gaze fixed on Jack's resting place, I grapple with the harsh truth that we, as climbers, willingly embrace the inherent risks of Everest. On the treacherous north side, beyond the daunting ascent of the notorious 2nd Step and deep into the unforgiving Death Zone, the slim chance of survival following a serious mishap looms over us like an ominous shadow.

Engrossed in contemplation and grappling with these dilemmas, I abruptly snap out of my wondering dream state, realising with a jolt that I'm drifting once more, losing precious focus. Exhaustion seeps through my bones, a constant companion in this unforgiving terrain, leaving me feeling not just physically drained but mentally scattered. The absence of supplemental oxygen exacerbates the relentless assault of high altitude, tightening its grip on my senses. Familiar symptoms surge forth: the inability to concentrate, a relentless urge to succumb to the enticing embrace of sleep. It becomes glaringly evident that survival hinges on my ability to wage war against these formidable adversaries.

I swallow two dexamethasone tablets, a steroidal-based altitude medication, hoping they will give me a kick and clear my mind, but I don't notice any effect.

I force myself up, feeling unsteady on my feet, turning to give Jack one last fleeting look before I continue my stagger down the mountain.

Every step is a battle against exhaustion, with each breath of this thin air a reminder that I'm still in the Death Zone. With my oxygen bottle long depleted, the mask serves no purpose, and I discard it, pulling it from my face. The harsh daylight pierces through the thin air; its rays scorch my exposed skin. My mind struggles to find focus amidst the chaos of fatigue, the clarity of thought clouded by the relentless demands of the mountain. Delirium begins to creep in, blurring the lines between reality and hallucination.

I press my crampons firmly into the icy slope beneath me, each spike biting into the unforgiving surface as I struggle to control my descent. Amidst the jagged rocks below, partially concealed by a thin veil of snow, I catch sight of a small ice cave. Squinting against the glare of the sun, I can make out the unmistakable outline of a figure huddled within. The cavity, barely a metre deep and two metres wide, offers scant refuge from the elements.

It's nice to finally see someone. As I approach, I start talking and explain to him, "I'm knackered," with a few sighs along with a few cough splutters.

The chap does not reply; I stare at him more closely, looking at his retro bright green boots, which look like ski boots. "Why the hell is wearing those things?" I think to myself. His boots look like a throwback to the 1980s. Only then do I release he is a long time dead. "Shit," I say to myself out loud. I really am getting delusional. I realise that he must have been here in this small cave for over 30 years.

With a heavy heart, I pivot to confront the mountain's daunting descent, knowing all too well that lingering any longer could seal my fate. After a brief pause, as if acknowledging an unwritten obligation, I address my companion and just say, "I'm heading down, getting out of here." Without a backward glance, I press forward, descending into the depths below.

It wasn't until months after returning home that I delved deeper into the literature surrounding Everest. It was then that I made a startling realisation: the individual I had conversed with was none other than the infamous "Green Boots." His presence, marked by his distinctive green boots, has served as a poignant landmark along the North Route of Everest for years.

I abstained from indulging in extensive readings of books and articles on Everest before embarking on the climb. This decision stemmed from the realisation that many mountaineering narratives tend to gravitate towards themes of mortality, which I thought would adversely affect my mental state before departure.

I later came across an article written by one of his family members expressing frustration at how Tsewang Paljor, from India, had been reduced to a mere object of fascination by many. His untimely demise during the descent from the summit adds a tragic layer to his story. Potentially, in the same storm in 1996 that was made famous on the Nepalese side by the book "Into Thin Air" or the Hollywood blockbuster, it was turned into "Everest".

Consider the profound notion that while watching the infamous 1996 disaster depicted in films or recounted in narratives, one can now envisage another struggle for survival unfolding concurrently on the opposite flank of Everest amidst the same stormy night.

Little did I realise that I too, was soon to endure my own Everest storm.

CHAPTER 18

The Storm

As I begin my descent down the steep rock face of the second step, I can't help but marvel at how different it appears in the daylight. During the arduous ascent in the darkness, which felt like an eternity ago, every ounce of my climbing experience was summoned to locate even the smallest handhold or foothold on the sheer rock. Now, in stark contrast, the descent feels almost serene as I smoothly abseil down the rope, effortlessly navigating the terrain. However, despite the newfound ease of movement, there's a distinct awareness of the 3,000-foot drop beneath me, serving as a constant reminder of the environment that surrounds me.

As I glance downward, I see Camp 3 in the distance. It's only about 300 metres below me, but I know it will take at least an hour to get there. I keep muttering to myself, "No stupid mistakes," as I feed the rope into my figure-of-eight abseil device, ready for the next 50 ft drop section. I fumble with my fingers, grappling to recall the intricate steps of feeding the rope through the device. As a seasoned climber, I had long relied on the familiar stitch plate for both belay and abseil. However, the unforgiving conditions of Everest demanded a departure from convention; the prospect of rigid, icy ropes necessitated adaptation to this larger, traditional abseil system.

The scattered array of orange and yellow tents at Camp 3 loom closer. What was the highest hell on Earth campsite to me only 18 hours ago now suddenly looks luxurious and one step closer to home.

A steep, snow-filled gulley lies between me and the camp. I decide to descend it by sliding on my back, a choice that, in hindsight, proves to be ill-advised. It's a stark reminder that complacency is creeping in. As I gain momentum, I realise this was not the wisest technique. I lose control on the treacherous slope and come straight into one of the tents, the sharp edge of my left crampon tearing through the thin fly sheet at the base of the tent. I sheepishly say, "Sorry," expecting a rush of people to come out; instead, there is just silence.

Surveying the scene at Camp 3, I'm struck by the audacious tilt of the modest tents perched precariously on the sheer mountainside. Tethered by mere ropes secured to mammoth rocks and ice stakes, their defiance against the gravity that beckons below is both astonishing and unnerving. One can't help but feel the impending threat of a potential plunge into the abyss thousands of metres beneath.

The illusion of security envelopes you as the ropes, acting like tentacles, anchor the camp, suggesting a sanctuary amidst the towering peaks. However, the looming threat of the next fierce storm serves as a stark reminder of the transient and precarious existence of these makeshift camps. Everest, ever commanding, is poised to reclaim this lofty territory, asserting her dominance once more as she does every year.

I use the last bit of my energy I can muster and remove my crampons. As I crawl into my tent, I collapse on top of my cold sleeping bag, immediately drifting into unconscious sleep.

I awake about two hours later, hearing talking in the tent next to me. Maverick and Max are making a move down. As we shout between tents, their final words to me are, "Don't sleep another night here."

I don't immediately answer, but then I call out to them, with my dry, husky voice, desperate for fluids, "Do you have any water?" I hear no reply. I mutter curses under my breath, a futile release of frustration as I confront the harsh reality of my oversight. The bitter realisation sinks in: I should have melted water earlier, anticipating this moment of dire need. It's been over twenty relentless hours, my throat parched, and my body drained of strength. The thought of venturing out to collect snow, struggling to rig up the stove, and then waiting patiently for it to melt the snow seems like an insurmountable task. I don't even know where the stove is.

"I have to move," I say to myself. As much as I don't want to do anything but sleep right now, I know Maverick and Max are right. I'm only degrading lying here, and another night at this altitude will probably finish me off.

I've lost track of Alex's whereabouts. His delay is unsettling, especially given the eerie silence enveloping the camp. It's as though I'm the sole inhabitant of this desolate landscape. What was once a sanctuary now bears the weight of a death camp. Every passing minute diminishes my hope of survival.

In the Death Zone, the human body begins a perilous decline. Already, my body instinctively redirects all available resources and blood flow to sustain vital organs, leaving my limbs drained of strength and my stomach unable to process nourishment. The countdown to total shutdown has begun; with every passing moment inches closer to the inevitable.

Despite enduring prolonged dehydration, an urgent need to relieve myself and have a wee grips me. Opting against the hard work of putting my crampons back on, I ventured just a couple of paces from the tent to relieve myself. However, as I begin to urinate, the soft, smooth rubber soles of my boots betray me, sending me crashing face-first onto the ice. I find myself slowly sliding down the steep slope of the mountain, one hand desperately clawing at the ice to halt my descent while the other shields my exposed privates from the abrasive ice.

This seemingly minor oversight of neglecting to secure my crampons, even for a brief moment to relieve myself outside the tent, tragically emerges as a major recurring cause of fatalities on the mountain. Countless climbers have ventured out for a quick pee, dismissing the need for crampons, only to meet a dire fate. They slip and vanish into the abyss, never to resurface again, lost to the ice crevasses below.

In a state of panic, I scramble desperately against the icy slope, acutely aware of the perilous consequences of my slip. With each futile attempt to gain traction, the reality of becoming another statistic in the annals of mountaineering tragedies looms closer. Pressing my body flat against the cold ice, I dig my fingers into the frozen surface, every movement a precarious battle against gravity. Miraculously, my descent halts just short of disaster, mere metres from where it began. With trembling hands, I claw my way back up, inch by inch. In a stroke of luck, I find purchase in a small pee hole in the ice, its edges softened by the warmth of my recent release. Gasping for breath, I finally reach the safety of the tent, the adrenaline-fueled panic giving way to a flood of self-reproach. As I hastily zip up my trousers, I curse my own recklessness.

I slowly put my crampons on. It takes ages, at least 20 minutes and then a further 10 minutes just to recover from the effort. Without supplemental oxygen, everything is ridiculously hard, and I'm still a bit shaken after my toilet mishap.

Just as I'm motivating myself to get moving, Alex comes stumbling through the tent. He is completely knackered and is slurring his words.

I tell him we need to get down. Alex, too tired to speak, just gives me a look that says he isn't moving. I wait another 30 minutes as Alex rests, then tell him it's time to go. He says he'll be right behind me. I noticed Alex had stashed a bit of water before heading for the summit. While he sleeps in front of me, I pull his bottle from his bag and take a big drink. The selfish drive to survive is ruling my decisions.

I start descending, aware that daylight is slipping away. My goal is to reach Camp 2 at 7,800 metres. This camp, situated below the North East Ridge, is also precariously perched on a mix of rocky outcrops and snow, making it the most exposed spot on the mountain. It's not ideal, but at 500 metres lower than Camp 3, it takes me below the Death Zone line of 8,000 metres.

Every piece of literature I encountered and every conversation I had emphasised the crucial point of not staying at Camp 3 for more than one night. The accounts of last year's failed expedition with Stephan, coupled with tales of his frostbite ordeal at Camp 3, were compelling enough for me to heed the warning. However, despite the warnings, Stephan inexplicably chose to spend two nights at Camp 3 on this summit attempt. This decision nearly resulted in the loss of all his toes.

Descending in a daze for three hours, I stumble upon what I believe to be my previous tent at Camp 2, though uncertainty clouds my mind as they all look the same. Without much thought, I select one and get inside. I'm too exhausted to care, and no one else is around anyway; I'm here alone. As I nestle into the tent, the sun fades behind the towering mountain, and darkness falls.

With nightfall arrives the biting cold, and despite cramming into my sleeping bag fully clothed, my sweat-soaked undergarments soon freeze solid. Lying there in darkness, my head torch depleted of battery power, I ponder my choice not to invest in an extra oxygen bottle. The absence of oxygen instils a genuine fear within me; the possibility looms that if I succumb to sleep, I may never awaken.

Lying there alone, I think to myself, "Where the hell is Alex? Did he follow me down? Is he out there in the dark?" Soon any fears or thoughts I have are overwhelmed with exhaustion as I drift off into a dreamless sleep.

Abruptly, I'm jolted awake, my senses assaulted by an intense wave of pain. Enveloped in darkness and disoriented, I struggle to comprehend my surroundings. My mouth is throbbing, and my face feels compressed. Lying there, bewildered and shocked, I attempt to work out my situation. Gradually, it dawns on me that the source of the pain in my mouth is a broken fibreglass tent pole that has crashed down on me. The fibre pole has splintered and is piercing my lip and gums. I recognise the familiar metallic taste of blood in my mouth again. I can't work it out. Has someone fallen on my tent? It feels like a tree has fallen over and is pinning me to the floor with its 10-ton weight squeezing the breath out of me.

My entire body is being crushed by an immense pressure. I'm immobilised, unable to draw breath, and consumed by a panic of confusion. Then, as if in response to my inner turmoil, the thunder roars, and the wind howls, as if confessing to their role in this ordeal.

I get a split second of comfort in the understanding of my current situation. However, with the wind howling at over 100km an hour, this feeling quickly evaporates, and the realisation of my predicament sets in. A real sense of dread overwhelms me as I think to myself, "I'm gonna get blown off this mountain."

What follows is undoubtedly the longest and most agonising six hours of my life. The relentless force of the wind presses the tent flat against the mountain, threatening to tear it from its precarious hold. It's not a matter of if, but when, my tent will be swept away like a kite into the night, carrying me unwillingly down the treacherous slopes of Everest, thousands of feet below.

I extract the fractured, sharp fibreglass tent pole from my bloody mouth and shift onto my right side in the pitch-black darkness. The tent's canvas envelops my face tightly, pressing my body harder against the icy ground. It feels as though the tent's fabric is moulding a plaster cast around me.

With the fabric tightly compressed around me, I'm certain my facial expression is visible from the outside, which is mostly fear. It's like the scene in "The Empire Strikes Back" when Han Solo got frozen in carbonite.

As I lay pinned down, I grope through the pitch black with my right hand, searching for my ice axe buried somewhere in the tent. The cold steel meets my fingertips, and I grasp it tightly. With painstaking effort, I begin to turn over onto my belly, but progress is slow. It feels as though the tent has me ensnared in the tightest bear hug ever. I manage to get my shoulder up so I can turn over. As I do this, the tent starts flapping wildly, almost as if I've upset it. I think to myself, "This is it; the tent and I are going off the edge." I muster the strength to raise the head of the ice axe a few inches off the ground. Gripping it tightly, I thrust the sharp point downward with all my might. The front edge pierces through the thin tent fabric, striking the ice beneath. I had hoped for a deeper penetration, but the axe only sinks about a centimetre into the ice.

It's a pretty rubbish effort, and I'm well aware that if the tent is blown off, this little grip on the ice won't save me. It feels like I'm barely hanging on, clinging by my fingernails. Yet, it's better than nothing, offering an impression of control, even if it's just an illusion.

As seconds turn into minutes and hours in the darkness, I dare not move, let alone sleep. Hunched over my ice axe, its silver steel teeth still embedded in the ice, the tent canvas keeps me immobilised. The relentless howling wind has become almost routine, and in the darkness, exhaustion creeps in, causing my mind to begin drifting.

My thoughts turn to home. What the hell was I thinking leaving my five-week-old, newborn son for this suicide mission?

For the past three years, I've been entirely focused on achieving my dream, ignoring the rational thoughts and emotions any new father would normally have. Now, lying in my battered tent, I can see the grim reality of Everest's 1 in 10 death rate unfolding before my eyes. It's only been hours since I witnessed Jack's death, and I can't shake the feeling that I'm next in line to become another statistic of Everest's hostile nature. What is wrong with me that I would take such a risk after just having my first son?

I had always joked, when asked about the dangers of Everest and the one-in-ten death rate, by spinning it around saying, "I have a 90% chance of surviving." Now, sitting alone in the storm high up on this mountain, the joke did not seem as funny anymore.

Alone in my tent, I attempt to rationalise everything by convincing myself that without my determination and sheer stubbornness, Everest would have remained an unattainable dream. Conquering the doubters and financial obstacles made each subsequent challenge seem achievable. However, as I pause for breath, a sudden realisation strikes me: I did see the birth of my first child as an impediment to my climb. Now, high on this mountain, the stark reality dawns on me that I may never lay eyes on my son Sam again.

In the five weeks from Sam's birth to my departure for Everest, my mind was consumed with packing and organising my climbing gear. Despite being physically present at home, my focus on these practical tasks served as a subconscious defence mechanism. It prevented me from becoming too attached to my newborn baby, fearing that such an attachment might loosen my nerve and lead me to reconsider my seemingly mad decision to attempt climbing this mountain.

With the storm on Everest only increasing in strength, I relive the last sad image of my wife and child waving me off in the rain when I had departed all those months ago.

I sensed it wouldn't be long before the wind tore out all the tent's anchor points. The way the tent flapped at its corners indicated only one or two anchors remained, with some already ripped out. As I lie here, I contemplate if I'm on my last anchor point. I think to myself, if that anchor gives way, it spells the end of this makeshift campsite, and I'll be blown over the edge.

In my contemplation of what I believe to be my final moments, I am overwhelmed by a blend of guilt and acceptance that it's all coming to an end. Amidst this turmoil, an urge emerges to leave a farewell message for Sam and my wife Abi, perhaps to be discovered with my body on the mountain someday. However, engulfed in darkness and devoid of pen and paper, I find myself unable to fulfil this impulse. At Base Camp, just before the summit push, I had already penned a goodbye note in my diary, but those words seemed empty now, lacking genuine sentiment. What I really wanted to say was sorry.

Six hours have elapsed, and my grip on the ice axe has weakened to a feeble, desperate clench, as if it could somehow prevent my inevitable fall. Memories drift in and out of my mind, blurred by moments of consciousness consumed by the relentless white noise of the wind.

Suddenly, I feel the tip of my ice axe moving; it no longer

has any purchase in the ice, the whole tent is moving. The last anchor point holding the tent has come loose. I'm bracing myself, thinking, "This is it," waiting to get blown off of the mountain. I frantically attempt to plunge the ice axe into the ground, but it refuses to bite into the ice, and the tent inches closer to the precipice. Panic sets in as I desperately try to halt my death slide, but my efforts are futile. Suddenly, the tent comes to an abrupt stop. Reduced to a mere piece of flapping material in the gale, it's held in place by its last remaining anchor point. I exhale a deep sigh of relief, grateful that one anchor remains to save me. I lie motionless, uncertain of the strength of this final anchor, unsure if it will be torn free at any moment.

It feels like an hour passes in this heightened state of fear, anticipating the tent's next slide. Normal sounds elude me amidst the relentless drone of the high-speed wind. My face numbs under the pressure of the tent canvas, offering scant protection from the biting cold, with a sense of powerlessness washing over me as my fate hangs in the balance. I've exhausted my reserves, feeling done.

In an abrupt instant, the relentless white noise ceases without warning. It's as if a switch has been flipped, and the wind recedes to a gentle breeze. The suffocating grip the tent has held on me for hours suddenly loosens, granting me freedom of movement once more. The near-silence that follows feels unfamiliar, requiring a moment to adjust. It's similar to the muted hush you experience after leaving a blaring nightclub in the early hours of the morning.

Only then, in the silence, do I realise I can see my white-knuckled hand limply clutching my ice axe. Daylight has come. For the second time on this summit attempt, the sun has saved me. Just when I thought all was lost in the darkest hour, the sun's rays gave me hope that I could make it down.

I fumble to find the zip to exit my ripped, flattened tent. As I look around the camp and see the storm's destruction, with many tents blown into the abyss and others flattened like pancakes, I think about the luck or chance that made me choose this tent. Although after the night I've just endured, I don't feel very lucky.

I inspect my demolished tent, noticing it's held in place by a single piece of rope still attached to its anchor point in the rock. The small steel piton, driven into the loose rock, has held fast. I tap the rock to see how solid it is but more out of a sense of appreciation, like an affectionate tap. Without this small 10cm piton securing the tent, we would have surely been blown off the mountain during the night. I use "we" when referring to my shredded tent, as it was more than just a piece of yellow canvas and fibreglass poles to me now; we had been through that night together, and it had saved me. To this day, I have a newfound respect for ensuring my tent, wherever I am, is properly pegged and anchored down.

It's around 7 a.m. The sun is up, and the early morning blue skies show no sign of the storm that battered us through the night. I sift through the remnants of my shredded tent and get my crampons, and then strap them on. I salvage my sleeping bag and stuff it into my rucksack, leaving behind my roll mat and whatever else spilled out during the night chaos.

I pause briefly, realising Alex must still be up at Camp 3. But I can't dwell on it. I need to get down to Camp 1, at 7,000m, where the cooking equipment is, so I can melt some snow. I'm massively dehydrated, and after all the rigours of the last few days, this one thing could be my undoing. I'm transfixed with getting a drink; the classic Mariner's tale, "Water, water everywhere nor any drop to drink," runs through my mind as I look at the hard snow and ice around me, dreaming of water.

I'm moving well down the mountain now; for every 100 metres of altitude I descend, I feel the extra oxygen in the air and the surge in energy that comes with it. It's an 800-metre descent from Camp 2 to Camp 1 and takes me about three hours.

I crash through the zip of my old tent at Camp 1. It seems this whole camp fared better in the storm last night.

I gather a bag of snow from around the outside of the tent and can think only of melting it to drink. I don't even stop to see what colour the snow is that I'm shovelling. The wise saying, "Never eat yellow snow," came to mind. The fact that we had been peeing around the tent before the Summit bid on the way up mattered not a bit at this point.

I then proceed to try and light the stove with my fumbling frozen hands, cursing whist burning my fingers with the matches in the process. Then, within 30 minutes, I'm quenching a thirst never experienced before with some of the best-tasting, lukewarm, yellow water I've ever had.

Relaxed and hydrated for the first time in a long while, I lie back in my now warm tent as the sun's rays penetrate the light-yellow canvas.

After dozing for an hour, I push myself up, conscious that the descent is still not over with the challenging North Col still to get down. I pack the last of my gear in my bag and get ready to go.

Descending from Camp 1 at 7,000 metres means tackling the North Col ice face, a steep, 400-metre cliff riddled with crevasses. The initial section is the most daunting, featuring a nearly vertical 40-metre drop that plunges directly towards what seems like a bottomless crevasse. I choose to abseil this section and recall saying over and over to myself, "Check the knot, don't die now," referring to my belay abseil device.

I'm slow but trying to be methodical. Too many mistakes have already happened higher up. I am determined not to let drifting thoughts be the cause of another accident.

After fifteen minutes, I carefully cross the nearly horizontal aluminium ladder spanning the 10-metre crevasse. Safely across, I start to pick up pace, feeling excitement brewing. In the distance, I see Crampon Point, the place where I can finally remove my climbing equipment and leave the ice behind.

I eventually reach Crampon Point, where a Sherpa hands me a can of coke. It's a stark contrast from where I was just a few hours ago, battling the dark storm. Sitting here now, in relative safety, feels like a distant memory. As I sip my victory Coke, I sense a profound shift within me. A weight has been lifted, and for the first time in ages, I feel a surge of relief washing over me. The fear that gripped me has dissipated. The burden I've carried since my arrival has vanished. For the first time in a long time, I truly believe that I might actually survive this.

Max, who arrived before me, then instantly ruins the mood by saying, "Where's your buddy?" He was making the point that I was no longer with Alex, my Summit night companion. It was a fair question, one to which I didn't have a precise answer. I clarified that he hadn't descended with me from Camp 3. Max repeated it, this time in a critical tone, suggesting that I had abandoned Alex.

The expectation to stick together with your climbing partner for mutual support doesn't always hold true in reality. Despite our best intentions, Alex and I found ourselves separated multiple times, including during the descent from Camp 3, due to our differing climbing speeds and occasional miscommunication. Alex had spent a difficult night at Camp 3, opting to rest rather than descend.

I refuse to let Max's comments spoil my mood. A profound sense of relief washes over me that the end of this ordeal is within reach. After enduring last night's hardships, everything else in life seems manageable. No challenge will ever compare to that. Today isn't the day I meet my end; it's the day I'm going home.

CHAPTER 19

Milk Pee

You would think that after you have just summited the highest mountain in the world and that you are now safe back at Base Camp you will be on a high. I was for about half a day.

After the long 21km trek down from Advanced Base Camp to Base Camp, it's a great feeling knowing that you don't have to go back up again. However, it was very short-lived.

Within half a day of reaching Base Camp, I hit rock bottom. The weight of impending death and the relentless physical strain of the mountain had drained me completely, leaving me a now skinny, exhausted man struggling even to get out of his tent.

I intentionally gained weight before embarking on my Everest journey, anticipating the inevitable weight loss. I diligently consumed excess calories, striving to add three stone in the months leading up to it. Gaining weight, particularly for endurance events, is more challenging than one might imagine. Intense training regimes demand significant calorie expenditure, complicating weight gain efforts. Despite these hurdles, I succeeded in starting my expedition weighing 15 and a half stone.

In high altitudes, the body undergoes significant strain due to reduced oxygen levels, leading to increased calorie burn even during sleep compared to home. Coupled with the strenuous physical exertion of climbing and altitude-related symptoms like loss of appetite, I experienced rapid weight loss. Upon reaching Base Camp post-summit, I had shed 5 stone, nearly a third of my body weight, bringing me down to 10 and a half stone. While my visibly prominent rib cage marked a significant change, it wasn't the most alarming alteration to my physiology.

Sleeping in the tents at night, the temperature outside can drop to -25 degrees. With these temperatures, you don't want to get out in the middle of the night to pee, so you use a special bottle to relieve yourself inside the tent.

Feeling utterly drained at Base Camp that first night upon returning from the Summit, I refilled my urine bottle without any issues during the night. However, when daylight broke the next morning, I was horrified to find the bottle filled with a substance resembling milk. I couldn't comprehend how I had managed to expel what seemed like a pint of milk. The revelation left me deeply unsettled. Upon discussing the matter with Seb, who possessed medical expertise, he explained that once the body depletes its carbohydrate and fat reserves, it proceeds to metabolise proteins, resulting in the urine turning white. Essentially, my body had initiated self-cannibalisation, beginning to consume my own muscle tissue.

With my body now severely depleted, I knew I had to start eating again. Fortunately, luck was on my side as the Swiss team had organised a substantial post-summit party at Base Camp.

With most climbers enduring two and a half months in freezing conditions on the mountainside, with limited food, any party offering a banquet with booze was bound to go wrong.

The Swiss team had an impressive set-up at Base Camp on the north side, boasting a massive geodesic tent capable of accommodating 50 or 60 people comfortably. True to their reputation for precision and thoroughness, the Swiss had planned every aspect of their expedition, including ample provisions of party food and booze, well in advance of their departure. Although the Swiss team hadn't explicitly extended an invitation to us, we decided to join them nonetheless.

Imagine then, to our delight, that after a principal diet of noodles, eggs and rehydrated food for the last few months, we were tantalised with an array of cold-cut salami and meats from the finest charcuterie in the Alps. Next to a table full of French, Italian and Swiss cheeses, twenty different types of dessert with fresh fruit are laid out in a mouth-watering display. It felt a little surreal being surrounded by all of this, especially due to my physical appearance. I had a crazy beard and matted hair and although wearing my best outfit, my clothes were a bit dirty. With my current severe weight loss and eyes bulging from my skinny face, I felt more like a homeless crack addict who had crashed a wedding reception. I did, however feel in good company, as Alex and a few others from the other expedition groups also looked pretty dishevelled, making me feel right at home.

The table before us showcased an opulent display of food arranged in a staggering manner that resembled an artistic sculpture, especially with the stacks of meat. Despite the lavishness of the spread, the Swiss organisers made one critical error. They allowed the hungry climbers unrestricted access to the buffet, with no one serving out portions. In an instant, animal instincts took over, and it turned into a chaotic feeding frenzy. With only one overwhelmed Sherpa attempting to maintain order at the Salami end of the table, he was quickly overrun by the ravenous crowd, eager to gorge themselves on the banquet. I found myself with a chicken leg dangling from my mouth, only to catch the disapproving gaze of the Swiss host. Pausing briefly, I resumed my chewing.

What was essentially food for 70 people was consumed by about 20 of us.

I do recall saying thank you at the end, but it appeared lost on the Swiss host as he looked very disappointed and chose not to answer me.

I reminded myself not to feel too bad as it was only that morning I had seen my milk pee, so I justified my dinner antics with a medical reason.

After filling their bellies, most of the raiders sat down for the first time in 15 minutes, feeling slightly sick from overeating. The Swiss host attempted to reassemble the small remains of the food on the table to its former glory. Realising the damage was too great, he conceded and decided to join us.

Not only had the Swiss provided a very nice spread of food but they had also been kind enough to bring a staggering selection of alcohol, including beers, fine wines and spirits.

As the evening progressed and the drinks began to flow, the atmosphere around the table became livelier. After a few beers and bottles of wine had their corks popped, we started sharing stories of triumphs and defeats from the climbing season on the mountain.

Some teams had delayed their summit attempts by a day and got caught in the same storm I encountered on my descent, failing to reach the top. Despite this, they were in good spirits, knowing they would soon be heading home like the rest of us in the next few days.

Across the dining area, I spot a slim climber standing alone. I beckon him over, motioning with the bottle of red wine I've stolen. As I pour him a glass, I realise it's Uli Steck, the legendary speed climber.

Though Uli is Swiss, and the party is hosted by the Swiss team, he is also a gate crasher and gratefully accepts the stolen wine. He explains he's trying to complete as many speed climbs as possible while he's here.

While talking about his attempt on another 8,000m peak, Uli downplayed his achievement. He mentioned the tough descent but didn't highlight that he had just completed the fastest solo speed ascent of the mountain. He then moved on to his Everest summit attempt from the north side. He explained that he had carried minimal gear to climb quickly, but his feet got too cold, forcing him to turn back before reaching the summit due to the fear of frostbite. I mentioned that I remembered seeing a man hobbling past me, and we both laughed.

I'd had a few too many wines by then and started talking about Jack's death, but Uli didn't respond much. In my alcohol-filled mind, paranoia set in. Maybe he knew I'd left Jack to continue my climb. I quickly changed the subject. I poured Uli more wine and started telling tales of the ridiculous antics of throwing poo around our campsite.

Uli tragically died near Everest a few years later, not on a particularly difficult section by his standards. Like many great climbers, you don't realise their impact until they're gone. I only had one night with Uli, but his climbing videos still leave me breathless with his daring and speed. I'm grateful for that brief moment with him.

Despite everyone telling stories at the party of their Everest exploits, it did feel like there was a big elephant in the room. Jack's death was glaringly absent. Everyone was definitely aware of his death, but it seemed purposely hidden from any conversation. My mind was filled with questions. Had they also been faced with the same dilemma as me? They must have had some experience with him if they summited on the same night. Was he dead by the time they passed him? Had he been moved off the route by that point? I did not know. What I did know was that everyone was going out of their way not to talk about it, and when the conversation drifted in that direction, it was abruptly steered to another topic or another drink conveniently poured. Again, my paranoia returned, thinking they knew something. Did they know I had left Jack that night to continue my summit bid? Was that why they didn't want to talk about it? Or perhaps they had their own skeletons they were trying to hide.

The truth was, everyone just wanted to let off steam and enjoy themselves. Regardless of their involvement in the tragedy, no one wanted to discuss it at the party.

The celebration continued long into the Himalayan night,

with the climbers becoming merrier by the minute. The hardships and horrors of the past two and a half months were left behind, and we were simply grateful to be alive.

Having your first few beers after returning from the mountain marks an important turning point. The weight that lifts when those first beers are poured signifies much more than just a drink. It's a signal that all the pain and hardship are over, that you are going home, and more importantly, that you are going home alive.

Never underestimate the power of that first beer. The positive energy in the room at that moment, after you've pushed yourself far beyond what you ever thought possible, both physically and mentally, is immense.

Whether celebrating in an African bar in Tanzania after summiting Kilimanjaro or at a Base Camp party after returning from Everest, the emotional buzz is undeniable. I've often thought that if you could bottle that moment, you would have the true essence of contentment and happiness. I often feel that this celebration is the real high point of any expedition, far surpassing the summit itself, which can feel underwhelming due to the immense expectations attached to it.

Knowing that you are returning home to family and friends victorious, with the fear of failure and death behind you, is an unparalleled feeling. Sharing a drink with the people who have cried and bled alongside you on this great adventure is a moment that's hard to rival in any other walk of life.

I think that's one of the reasons I keep coming back to expeditions. These moments of pure joy, seeing others so high, are incredibly addictive.

That night at the Base Camp party, as the beer and whisky flowed, all negative thoughts eventually vanished. I could finally bask in the warm glow of knowing I had reached the summit of Mount Everest.

The next day, with sore heads, we began dismantling the camp, preparing to return to civilisation. The carefree, jubilant atmosphere of the previous night's party was gone, replaced by a sense of apprehension about returning home. After so many months of wishing the whole ordeal to be over, when it actually arrived, and our departure was imminent, I could not really believe it.

As the sun set behind Mount Everest, I crawled into my cramped, yellow tent at Base Camp, knowing it would be my final night there. Trying to grasp the reality that my journey was over, I flipped through the pages of my diary, each day dutifully crossed out, confirming the end of my expedition.

On a night that would be expected to be satisfying, sleep eluded me. I tossed and turned in my sleeping bag, haunted by the memories of summit night. The first of many nightmares began, replaying the horror of that fateful ascent. I vividly recalled the moment when I struggled to free my foot from the grip of a dying man.

With this nightmare haunting my weary mind, I couldn't view Everest as merely another accomplishment to tick off and move on. Something had shifted within me. These selfishly driven pursuits now prompted me to question their true purpose. It seemed as though I had reached a point where I no longer felt the need to prove anything.

By the time the sun rose for the last time on my frozen tent, a new anxiety starts to burn within me. How am I to return home and tell my Everest tale with the dark truth that night? How will I be judged, and what price have I yet to pay?

After loading all our gear into the 4x4 vehicles, we embarked across the Tibetan plateau. Despite months of anticipation for this moment of escape, I found myself staring blankly through the dusty window, my gaze fixed on the distant horizon. However, instead of excitement, a sense of fear crept over me about my impending return.

CHAPTER 20

Home

After returning home from Everest, I felt utterly drained. What should have been a time of celebration, reuniting with family, and basking in my triumph turned out to be quite the opposite. For three long years, I had a singular, unwavering mission: to conquer Everest. Now that I had achieved it, a sense of being lost and emptiness crept in. Despite the comforting familiarity of being back home, everything seemed surreal and detached. With so many questions rattling around my head, I needed to now acclimatise to my new home environment. What do I do now? Do I just return to the day job of policing and get back into playing happy families? I understood deep down that it wouldn't be straightforward. Whenever solitude enveloped me, my mind wandered to a cold, dark place on the mountainside. It felt as though Everest hadn't released its grip on me just yet.

As the weeks started to go by at home, interest began to build within my home town of Bristol about my Everest climb. I was being billed as "The first Bristolian to climb Everest". With this came lots of local media interest and interviews, all probing to get the inside scoop on the story. Jack's demise on Everest had become public knowledge, sparking numerous inquiries directed at me. I provided bits of information concerning my involvement in the incident but consistently skirted around the actual events. However, my attempts to downplay my role only heightened curiosity, leading to more questions. So much so that I started to get worried that it was just a matter of time until potential accusations would start to come my way.

By far, a death on Everest invariably gains more attention and tends to sell more papers. My guarded approach, refraining from providing a comprehensive account of all the circumstances surrounding the incident, allowed certain individuals to speculate and fill in the gaps with their own imagination and version of events.

Online has always been a haven for those to air and share strong opinions, with little concern of reprisals, so it was here that my deepest fears came true.

I was certain that delving too deeply into the complexities of mountaineering would only invite severe criticism, making me vulnerable. Hence, I opted to keep it simple, stating that I had continued my climb, passing someone in distress who later died. Ironically, my minimal disclosure backfired, fuelling resentment as unfounded speculations arose to fill the void.

What still strikes me today is the sheer volume of opinions surrounding the matter. Most vehemently condemned the act of leaving a dying man behind to pursue one's selfish climbing ambitions, regardless of the circumstances. They were so convinced of their righteousness, hurling a barrage of abuse my way.

Initially, I made the mistake of engaging in online debates, hoping to justify my actions. However, I quickly realised it was futile and only exacerbated the situation. It seemed as though I had personally offended them, with any attempt at defence met with hostility.

With this all taking place within the first two months of returning, it did nothing to assist my transition back into normal life. It's as if those hypothetical debates on the "Hero Complex" we had had as a team on Everest to pass the time were coming to life. Although I knew the facts were very different, these negative accusing comments directed at me started to get into my head. Had I left a man to die?

CHAPTER 21

Devil in the Death Zone

Despite the intense scrutiny following my Everest climb, it soon faded into old news, and my critics receded. I began to slowly reintegrate into everyday life, balancing my work in the police with my new role as a father. During this time, I continued to give public talks on Everest and motivational seminars, speaking in various settings, from schools to large corporations.

My talks would cover the rigours of overcoming the hardships of Everest, spinning the idea of using these lessons to tackle everyday problems. However, I would only briefly touch on the true events of that summit night, mentioning the death briefly to add some dramatic twist to the talks. I recounted the same speech so often that these tales started to replace my true memories of the actual events. My mind seemed content to adopt and believe the new storyline, almost happy to disregard the part of me that had shown its dark, selfish side that night on the mountain.

With my denial of those events buried deep within, I allowed myself to embrace the rewards of reaching the top of Everest. Any criticism of my conduct that night seemed long forgotten, and my public talks painted me in a positive light. Now, I had credibility with an audience eager to join me on new adventures.

This newfound status and acceptance gave me the confidence to start my own mountaineering trek business, leaving my job in policing to forge a new path. If I were to continue with more adventures, it couldn't be on the same selfish terms as before. I needed to earn money for my family and involve them in my travels, not just spend it on my own pursuits.

By using the foreign contacts I had gathered over the years as a mountain guide, I began organising my own adventure trips worldwide. From the jungles of Borneo to the Peruvian Andes, many people were eager to join my new expeditions. It seemed that the physical and financial risks of climbing Everest had finally paid off.

The difference between being a police officer and running my own international adventure business could not be more contrasting. While both roles involve significant risk management and problem-solving, they are vastly different. Policing, 99% of the time, involves dealing with problematic sectors of society. Whether it's drugs, violence, fraud, or murder, a police officer's day-to-day life immerses you in the worst that people have to offer. Although you do get to help victims, your role is limited after the initial enquiry. You have little to no contact with the victim once the case goes to court, so you rarely know the outcome of your work. This makes the job seem unrelenting, as you constantly deal with the same negative individuals who cycle in and out of prison, offering little reward or optimism for your efforts.

After 15 years of dealing with the darker side of society, it's easy to see how a police officer's outlook can become cynical and negative, affecting those around them. This was true for me as the cynicism began to creep in.

In stark contrast, leading a group on an adventure of a lifetime, whether up a mountain in the Himalayas or down a river rapid in the Borneo jungle, has the opposite effect. The pure excitement and sense of achievement the clients experience is infectious. Over the years, these positive experiences have transformed me and my outlook on life.

After a few years, my expedition company was thriving, expanding into numerous mountain ranges worldwide and creating bespoke adventures. The heroic narrative of my Everest tale was now firmly etched in my mind, and the events of that fateful night seemed buried. However, like a sleeping giant, those disturbing, suppressed memories were soon to be reawakened.

A short while after Everest, I led a group of 25 police officers to the summit of Kilimanjaro. Though this was one of many trips I had guided on this mountain, Kilimanjaro's challenges were not to be underestimated. Despite being classified as a trek, its nearly 6,000-metre height poses serious risks. Each year, altitude-related issues lead to numerous fatalities.

During this trip, on descent from the summit of Kilimanjaro, a client of mine, Peter, encountered severe altitude complications and tragically collapsed and died. This event marked one of the most harrowing experiences of my life. I was confronted not only with the daunting task of retrieving Peter's body from the mountain but also with the responsibility of calming the fears of the remaining group, who were now acutely aware that one of their companions had died.

We carried Peter's body down from the higher altitudes to a point where we could place him on a makeshift stretcher, a steel frame with a motorbike wheel in the middle. This wheel allowed us to roll the body downhill, but it involved an exhausting five-hour balancing act to manoeuvre it over the steep terrain. Occasionally, the wheeled stretcher would break free, leading to frantic chases to catch it before it gained too much speed. Despite the difficulties, the descent from Kilimanjaro didn't compare to the high-altitude, steep ice slopes of Everest. By the end of the day, I managed to get Peter to the base of the mountain.

Strangely, just before his untimely demise, I captured a photograph atop Kilimanjaro during sunrise. Assuming the stance of a cross-like figure, I extended my arms, casting a silhouette against the backdrop of the awakening African sun, creating an unintentional semblance of a crucifix. What initially seemed like an artistic shot to promote my website would later, hauntingly, coincide with the precise location where my trekker tragically collapsed and succumbed to his fate three hours later.

Although it was sudden and unexpected, with no signs that he was in any difficulty, this was still my Kilimanjaro trip and, therefore, my responsibility.

The aftermath of assuming leadership and bearing the weight of responsibility for a death during this expedition brought about a profound and challenging ordeal. The intense scrutiny endured both during and after the incident tested me in ways I had never imagined. It compelled me to do a thorough examination not only of my protocols and decisions but also demanded a deeper inner search, urging me to confront the harsh realities of how events unfolded on Kilimanjaro and whether any positives could be learned. Through an in-depth analysis, it became evident that this tragedy was an unfortunate occurrence beyond anticipation or prevention.

The deep dive into my thoughts prompted by the Kilimanjaro incident yielded an unforeseen revelation. It started a journey of self-discovery, unearthing the raw emotions and untold truths of my harrowing experience on Everest. Gradually, I began to unravel the tangled web of denial and self-comforting that had buried my real Everest memories for the last few years.

It's ironic that it took this second death on Kilimanjaro to reveal the truth of how I really felt about the first.

The dormant memories and suppressed emotions from that fateful night on Everest surged back with an overwhelming force, as if the protective barrier of denial had been blown away. Suddenly, I found myself confronted with the unvarnished truth of the incident that had transpired years ago. The weight of guilt that now bore down on me stemmed not merely from the impossibility of saving Jack's life, for he had reached a point beyond rescue, but rather from the haunting realisation that I had abandoned him in his final moments of struggle. This was compounded by the fact that, at the time, I had also felt elated that I could continue with my climb, not caring about any later consequences. The vivid image that now sears my mind is that of me turning my back on the helpless man lying at my feet, consumed by a selfish sense of relief as I forged ahead with my climb.

It's as if I was now seeing my Everest climb in full vivid technicolour. From the harsh reality of the gruelling efforts to raise funds to the selfish decisions made on the mountain, I found myself questioning whether the sacrifices made in its conquest had truly been worth it.

Climbing Everest has undoubtedly unlocked new opportunities, propelling me into running my own expedition company that has taken me all over the globe. Yet, beneath this success lies a darker truth, one I cannot ignore. For those thinking of going down my path, it would be negligent of me not to tell the true tale and reveal the deal I made with the Devil that fateful night to conquer the summit at any cost. Years later, I have to pay the price as the Devil comes back into my nightmares to claim his end of the bargain. The price of guilt for my remaining days.

In the dangerous act of high-altitude mountaineering, the grim realities surrounding fatalities are too often missing within books that talk about triumph and glory. Yet, the true toll of these tragedies extends far beyond the icy slopes, lingering as a heavy burden of remorse and unanswered questions. The weight of guilt, borne by those who survive, is a constant companion, haunting their thoughts with relentless speculation over alternate choices and potential outcomes for the lives that are no longer with us. As if to deepen the anguish, I later discovered that Jack left behind a pregnant wife, poised to welcome another new life into the world. He was never to find out if it was a boy or a girl.

And so now I find myself looking back and questioning my decisions. Years on from these events and now, with more experience, would I have made different choices?

Perhaps a rescue attempt in the Death Zone during that chilling night might have ensured the safe return of us both, reuniting us with our families now. Yet, the grim reality suggests a different outcome: the likelihood of none of us surviving the descent, leaving me to face the same fate: a cold, lonely death amidst the remote Himalayan wilderness.

The uncertainty of that night's events and the subsequent judgment passed by others will forever remain beyond my grasp. Yet, what remains true is the enduring imprint left by such experiences. The spectre of death and tragedy, intrinsic to my mountaineering career, resurfaces years later in the dead of night. The figure I encountered, the Shadow Man, on that fateful night, seems to beckon once more, urging me to forsake him and press onward to the summit. Like an unresolved debt, his presence returns unbidden. He rouses me from restless slumber in a cold sweat to the screams and groans of a confused dying man. High on a dark mountain side, I gaze into the scared eyes staring straight through me, almost searching for help.

Within these moments, awakening in fear from these reoccurring nightmares, I have time in the early hours to ponder what I would do if given a second chance. Would I sacrifice my attempt to summit Everest and risk all the odds of a rescue?

As I search my soul, asking myself who I really am, my mind whispers a dark truth. Faced with this summit decision once more, high in the Death Zone, I would again choose to make my deal with the Devil.

Everest Myth Busters

- **There is litter everywhere up to Base Camp and beyond!**
  Everest, for many years now, has cleared up its act regarding litter and waste. The trek to Base Camp in Nepal is pristine, and you are hard-pressed to find any litter.

- **The Sherpas drag you up!**
  Although it is well documented that the role of the Sherpa in climbing Everest is invaluable when it comes to laying the fixed lines and carrying supplies, every climber has to physically climb themselves, and no one can be carried or pulled up.

- **Everest is like a conveyor belt with traffic jams.**
  Although it's fair to say that Everest has become more popular over the years, it still has relatively few people trying to climb it each year compared to other more accessible mountains. Sensational pictures of long queues would like to depict that it's the norm when climbing Everest; however, this does not happen often and is normally due to a good weather window opening up, causing a more than normal surge in climbers at the same time.

- **Everest is not the hardest mountain to climb.**
  Everest is not the most technical mountain out there, and K2, along with others, is more challenging. However, the sheer height of Everest, standing considerably taller than its nearest rival K2, makes the altitude on Everest a deadly factor.

- **Anyone can climb Everest these days. It's so commercial.** Yes, through the commercialisation of mountaineering in general over the years, the numbers and types of people attempting to climb Everest have changed. This, however, does not mean they all succeed, and many without sufficient prior experience fail or sadly account for the deaths.

- **Everest is so much easier to climb now than back when Hillary summited it in 1953.** Although climbing gear, clothing and technology have made mountaineering safer over the years, Everest is still at the same height it's always been, and it is still a formidable challenge. (NB, the Himalayas tectonic plates that formed the mountains are still colliding, so Everest is actually growing in height by a couple of centimetres a year.)

- **Doing Everest with oxygen is the easy way to do it.** It's a myth that you are breathing pure O2. You only have a limited supply of supplemental oxygen, and this mixes with the existing thin oxygen from the air in the mask bag, meaning it only partially assists you. Despite this help, everything is exhausting.

- **The north side of Everest is more dangerous.**
  The statistics of surviving Everest and getting home alive have varied over the years from over 10% fatality rate down to under 3 %. These statistics can sadly be transformed by a major incident such as the one that happened with the ice fall disasters in the last decade. I think it's fair to say that both the North and the south side of Everest have their own unique challenges to allow you passage to reach the highest point on Earth.

Classic Trek Quotes

Over the years of leading thousands of clients in the mountains to reach their summit goals, I have been fortunate enough to meet an amazing array of different people, making the experience worthwhile. Below are some comments made by trekkers that have stuck in my head.

"Do those glaciers get bigger the closer you get to them?"
Exhausted trekker not thinking straight.
Everest Base Camp 2010.

Asked in a very polite and calm manner, *"Dom, do you mind if I borrow the Sat phone to call a helicopter as I think I'm having a heart attack?"*
Dr Ramesh, the team Doctor, Louboche 4,700 metres, was flown back to Kathmandu for a triple bypass and made a full recovery.
Everest Base camp trek 2014.

"I didn't bother bringing a waterproof jacket as I knew there was no need for it. Looks like I was right!"
A cock sure trekker who, on descending from the summit after his comments, got caught in a major storm and went hyperthermic.
Mount Toubkal, 4,123 metres Morocco.

"Is he ok? Is he supposed to look like that? he looks very pale, and he is not moving his eyes. I've asked him if he wants some of my power bars as he looks like he needs a pick me up," the reply to which "No, I don't think that will help, he's dead."
A trekker from another team had sadly died days earlier of altitude-related issues and was still awaiting recovery.
2018 High Andes trek over 5,000 metres.

Asked an executive corporate client who needed fitting for climbing boots and crampons what his shoe size is, reply, *"I've no idea; I've never known my shoe size; my family's shoe cobbler takes care of all that."*
Cotopaxi 6,000 metres, Ecuador 2016.

Trekker in the Borneo Jungle has an itchy, inflamed eye. Later on in the day, I asked what might have caused it, and he stated very quietly, *"Earlier, when we were looking up at the Orangutans in the trees, one of them urinated on my face."* I tried to make light of it by saying that he was very lucky to get a golden shower from an Orangutan.
Borneo Jungle Expedition 2018.

Acknowledgements

This short book took much longer to write than anticipated, bringing up many buried emotions. So I must acknowledge the patience of my wife Abi and two boys Sam and Luc for giving me the space and time to finish it.

Thanks to my friend Ali Collacott-Nuur for his help with the first drafts and support throughout.

Those in the Police and Army that assisted with certain chapters.

I'd like to thank Humphrey Joram my Masi guide on Kilimanjaro Tanzania who trusted me from the very beginning when setting up the company Dom Pickett Expeditions and has been part of its growth ever since.

My Peruvian friend "ok lets go" Elkin – RIP

Geljin Sherpa and Shiv Raj Thapa who have offered me a wealth of experience and knowledge on all the expeditions I have run in the Himalayas.

Paul Murphy who acted as a friend and business mentor in the early days placing his trust in me and getting me through the hard times.

Fiona Dodsworth-Haag who took a chance and gave me the opportunity to lead my first Kilimanjaro expedition that got me started.

Simon Edwards for his help setting up my website, DomPickett.com, for free when I was just starting out

Clive Parfitt for his help in guiding the early drafts of the book

My life long friends Justin, Joe and Nick who have always been there over the years, with thanks to Joe for help on the final edit.

To the team I climbed Everest with, despite the tensions we succeeded.

To my Mum and Dad, brother Remi and sister Jenny for instilling a sense of adventure in me at such a young age that ultimately started me on the path to Everest.

Lastly to those that in their pursuit of adventure are no longer with us, Jack and Peter.

Picture acknowledgements

Eric P (Oregon), Dr Biff Palmer, Scot Patch, Ed Buckingham

Our International team, all smiles at the beginning of the Expedition.

Author bio

Dom started his adventures climbing in the Himalayas at an early age before returning to the UK to complete his degree in Business Management and Ethics at Leeds. Dom then tried various different career roles in the Army and Police before coming back to his mountaineering and trekking routes where over the last 15 years he has established his own worldwide adventure company, *Dom Pickett Expeditions*. Now a husband and father of two based in Bristol, England, Dom has found his true calling taking those seeking adventure to all corners of the Earth.

www.DomPickett.com

Printed in Dunstable, United Kingdom

83019828R00122